Light the candle — let it glow — and let your Wild Woman free with these pages.

MISS YOU

Love,

—JoAnne

CREATIVE WILDFIRE

CREATIVE WILDFIRE

AN INTRODUCTION TO ART JOURNALING—BASICS AND BEYOND

BEVERLY MASSACHUSETTS

QUARRY BOOKS

L. K. LUDWIG

First published in the United States of America by
Quarry Books, a member of
Quayside Publishing Group
100 Cummings Center
Suite 406-L
Beverly, Massachusetts 01915-6101
Telephone: (978) 282-9590
Fax: (978) 283-2742
www.quarrybooks.com
Visit www.Craftside.Typepad.com for a behind-the-scenes peek at our crafty world!

Library of Congress Cataloging-in-Publication Data

Ludwig, L. K.
  Creative wildfire : an introduction to art journaling basics and beyond / L.K. Ludwig.
      p. cm.
  Includes index.
  ISBN-13: 978-1-59253-601-6
  ISBN-10: 1-59253-601-8
  1. Handicraft. 2. Diaries--Authorship. I. Title.
  TT157.L82 2010
  745.5--dc22

                                                        2009052446
                                                        CIP

ISBN-13: 978-1-59253-601-6
ISBN-10: 1-59253-601-8

10 9 8 7 6 5 4 3 2 1

Design: Traffic Design Consultants
Book layout: Claire MacMaster, barefoot art graphic design / deepwater-creative.com
Illustrations: Judy Love
Photography: Lightstream / www.lightstreamns.com

Printed in China

begin artistic passion

We catch fire

smoldering at first we begin to explore, stumble upon the materials. And then triggered by gasoline wildfire! We

CONTENTS

INTRODUCTION

When I found my way, when I discovered that art was my passion, the experience was much like finding my voice. Although this might sound somewhat hokey, it's true. I fell head over heels in love with the process of learning and making art.

I first discovered the idea of using books as an art surface in a class I took, in which each student was required to bring artwork to discuss. One of the students, a painter, had found an old hardback book, written in Dutch, in a New York City phone booth. I remember her sitting in the middle of the conference table, showing us this book, whose pages she had filled with marks made with sticks of oil paint—little explorations of line and shape and color. The pages weren't primed, so the paint would eventually eat through the paper, and the thick marks never dried. The book was her fail-safe, and she brought it to class when she had no other work to show. I thought it clever and fascinating. The heady scent of oil paint and the sound of the waxed paper, tucked between the pages so they wouldn't adhere to each other, being pulled away as she turned the pages came together with my childhood love of books and paper, and the experience forever changed how I work. I discovered books as a surface to receive image and color, line and shape.

Being able to speak in the paper pages of books and on canvas with color, image, and words was transformational for me—like catching fire. Like a wildfire, but far kinder, each new technique, each new idea, sparked my creativity, causing a surge in my work. Of course, just like real fire, at times my work level burns down, becomes low and smoldering, sometimes only embers, until a new idea or brisk wind comes along and sets my work burning merrily once again.

This book has a dual purpose. One is to provide the basic fodder for starting new fires, information for those who are just beginning the process of keeping an art journal. More than a simple how-to, this book illustrates ways of working with both art mediums and the internal art-making process. The second purpose of this book is to provide sparks for existing fires by offering useful techniques, tips, and insights for those already familiar with art journaling. Throughout this book, I'll provide glimpses into the journals of other artists who share insights into the ways they approach their work.

I asked each of our contributors why art journals appeal to them. Their answers were surprisingly similar: Working in a private journal gives them the freedom to explore new approaches and personal topics. Many of the artists appreciated the ability to record their personal history or tell a story—to become authors and illustrators within their journals.

Join us, and discover how to use art journaling as a way to set fire to your sense of artistic play.

This journal, whose dual covers open like French doors, offers a dynamic art journal form because each time you open the book, a different view is possible.

CHAPTER 1:

GATHERING FUEL: HOW TO GET STARTED

What's an art journal? An art journal is a space, most often a traditional book, that houses a collection of artwork created on blank pages that are really journal entries. The journal entries, while primarily visual, can explore the full range of an artist's experiences: day-to-day life, personal growth issues, life-changing experiences, explorations of new artistic mediums, or simple stories. Pages of an art journal can be covered in paint, collaged with scraps of paper, used to highlight photographs, or showcase drawings. And, while an art journal page may or may not have text to narrate the content, it is the visual elements—paintings, drawings, photographs, and collages—that combine in an art journal page to communicate clearly what the artist has to say.

The basic fuel for our art journal creative wildfire consists of blank pages and art supplies: scraps and photos, words and thoughts. If you are an experienced art journaler, all you need to do is find a journal with some sturdy blank pages, pull out your art supplies, read through the techniques, decide what to try out first, and ignite!

If you have never done any art journaling, and are not sure how to begin, you may want to read through this book first to get an overview of the process. Your next step will be to choose a journal to work in. There are a plethora of art journal styles, and as you explore the process, you will undoubtedly discover some personal favorites that suit your way of working and the art mediums you choose. In this chapter, you'll find information on choosing a journal that is right for you, some commonly used types of art journals for various mediums, and techniques for making a journal of your own from scratch. One piece of advice: Pay attention to the journals shown in this book whose structure or format you are drawn to, and make a list of the type of journal structure they have. Ask yourself, what is it about the style that appeals to you? How does it suit the art mediums you like to use? Is it easily obtained? If you need a portable art journal, will that particular style of journal hold up under wear and tear? Choosing something you like that fits your working style will give you the best start. It is your time to gather information, and gather fuel to feed your own creative wildfire.

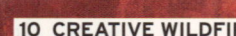

Karen Cole created this handmade portfolio folder out of art canvas and treated it as an art journal page by applying collage, writing, drawing, and painting across the entire surface.

CHOOSING A JOURNAL STRUCTURE

Before you apply images, color, or text to your journal pages, you should first decide on the structure of your journal. Choosing a journal can seem like a formidable process. Sketchbooks and journals are available in thousands of varieties, and when you include the possibilities open to you when you bind your own journal, the whole process becomes dizzying.

If you are new to the process of art journaling, choose an art journal that offers flexibility, such as a binder, portfolio, or scrapbook. These provide plenty of opportunity to experiment with different papers, mediums, and techniques.

If you're an experienced artist and know your journaling style and mediums of choice, create or purchase a journal with the paper and structure to suit your needs. A printmaker using prints in a journal, for example, will need a binder or portfolio, so the prints can be attached to the pages. Many journal artists keep multiple journals that vary in structure, paper, mediums used, and topics covered.

Overwhelmingly, our contributing artists preferred handmade journals, bound with sturdy paper of 140-pound or higher weight. Repurposing materials, such as cardboard, old envelopes, Tyvek, and paper grocery bags, to create pages was also popular.

A variety of books that can serve as great art journals: (A) black paper interleaved album (B) vintage record album (C) hand-bound book made with Braille paper (D) sketchbook with painted cover (E) wire-bound pad of watercolor paper (F) handbound journal with deckle edges, from Rag & Bone Bindery (G) handmade journal with binder rings used to house a journal of an artist's favorite paper (H) photo album ring binder (I) antique ledger

TIP

Although thick, juicy journals can be appealing to the eye, in practice, they can be daunting. The expectation of having to fill up all the pages can actually hinder your work. If you make your own journals, four signatures with three to four folios is a good size (see page 15 for more on signatures and folios). Don't hesitate to use fewer. If you're buying a journal, choose one with fewer pages, or remove some pages.

You can remove pages from a book with sewn-in signatures by tearing one or two folios (folded pairs of pages; see page 15) from each signature in the book. If you have chosen a book with glued-in pages, you will need to use a craft or utility knife with a fresh blade to remove pages. Be sure to cut pages from varying places to avoid a big gap in your book.

(A)

(B) *Record Album*

(C)

(F)

(E)

(D)

(G)

DAY BOOK

(I)

(H)

JOURNAL-MAKING BASICS

Pages Base your choice of paper for your pages on the mediums you will use in your journal and on your personal preference. Good-quality, sturdy paper can be found at various price levels. Although expensive 140-pound, cotton-rag watercolor paper might be appealing, less-expensive 140-pound, tablet-style watercolor paper, available at craft stores, will often suffice. A heavy drawing paper, such as Lenox, is less expensive than printmaking papers and will take acrylic paints nicely. Although working with expensive, quality paper can spur your work, it can also hinder your creativity, for fear of ruining the paper. Assess your needs, your hindrances, and your motivators and choose accordingly. You can always make a new journal, if you find your choice is unsuitable.

Covers Called *cover boards*, these can be made from Davey board, chipboard, cardboard from cereal boxes, canvas boards, Plexiglas sheets, or even metal. For easy, ready-made cover boards, just remove the front and back covers of an existing book. This is a good way to repurpose unwanted hardback books and to use a cover that inspires you.

This handmade journal uses the pages of a child's board book as a base structure. The covers were created using art canvas that has been previously painted and cut down to size.

SOME HELPFUL TERMINOLOGY

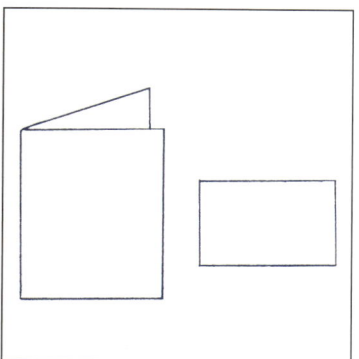

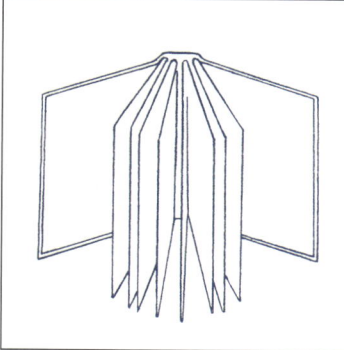

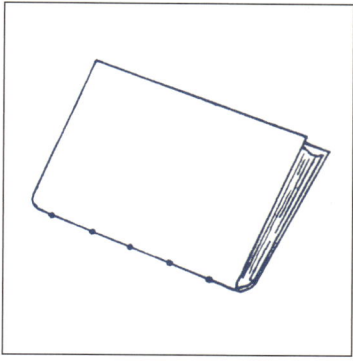

- **Folio**: a single sheet of paper folded in half.

- **Signature:** a group of sheets of paper folded in half (folios), nested together, that constitute one section of a book. For the instructions described, the size of your folio is determined by the size of your cover. Each of the unfolded sheets that becomes your folio should be the same height as one of the cover boards and twice its width.

- **Text block:** the group of signatures that is housed inside a book's covers. Most modern books are made by gluing the text block into the cover. In this book, we'll cover some traditional techniques for sewing signatures together to create a text block.

- **Sewing station:** the pierced holes along the spine of a folio through which the needle and thread enter and exit the folio spine. Where the pierced holes for the sewing stations are located is determined by the person binding the journal and is based on binding technique, journal structure, and personal taste. To ensure that the sewing stations align properly, a **template** for piercing the sewing stations in each folio is a necessity.

This journal was created by Mary Ann Moss for a trip to Italy. Built to be portable and flexible, she used sturdy chipboard covers and binder rings so the book could be opened and pages removed for working on easily while traveling.

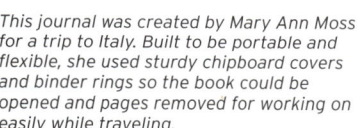

BINDING TECHNIQUES

Two useful binding techniques for art journaling are shown in this chapter. The first binding technique, the Sewn Over Tapes binding, uses a running stitch, which is simply sewing the needle into and out of the sewing stations and over fabric tape. The spine is exposed in this binding and lies flat when opened—a real advantage for journaling. The second binding technique also lies flat when opened. This binding technique, the Sewn Over Cords Binding with the Seed Pearl Stitch, uses a specific type of stitch to connect signatures to the sturdy cords that serve as the spine of the book.

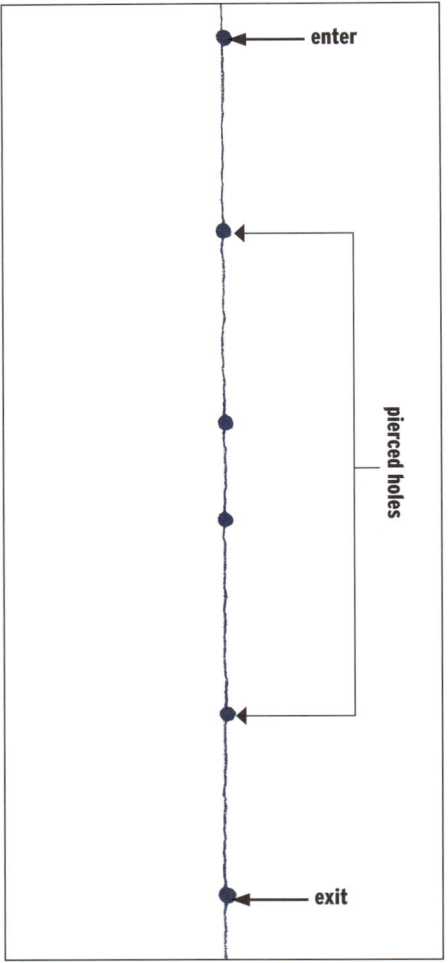

This diagram illustrates a sample template for piercing sewing stations. The diagram shows an entrance and an exit.

Making a Template for Piercing Sewing Stations

Materials

- scrap of paper the same height as one of your folios and 4" to 6" (10 to 15 cm) wide
- bone folder
- awl
- ruler
- pencil

1. Fold your scrap of paper in half lengthwise; crease hard with a bone folder.

2. Using a ruler and a pencil, mark your sewing stations. To help you locate the sewing stations, we've included illustrations with the Running Stitch binding and the Sewn Over Tapes binding instructions (see page 19). As you become more comfortable with binding techniques, you'll discover that you can vary the sewing-station locations to create interesting designs along the spines of your journals or to suit special needs. Some binding instructions require separate exit and entry holes along with the other stitches.

3. Pierce each hole with an awl. Then align this template with the inside of each signature and push the awl through the holes, being sure to pierce through the folios at each hole.

KETTLE STITCH DIAGRAM

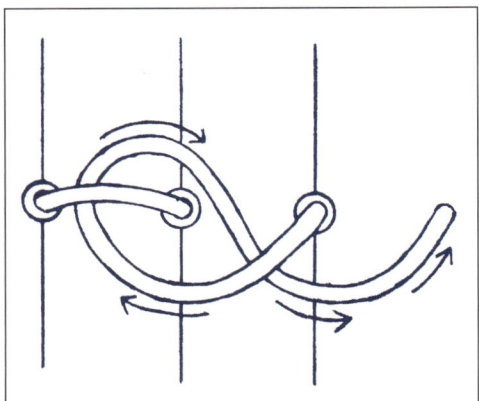

Kettle Stitch

For two of the binding structures in this book, a kettle stitch is used for the change-over stitch. A change-over stitch is the stitch that moves from the head and tail of one signature into the next signature. The kettle stitch is a common change-over stitch and is used for many sewn-binding techniques. You will use this stitch in the Sewn Over Tapes binding (page 17) and the Sewn Over Cords Seed Pearl binding (page 20).

1. When you have finished adding signatures one and two for your chosen binding technique, adjust the tension on the thread to be sure your binding is snug. Add the third signature in the same fashion.

2. At the end of the third signature, and before you add the fourth signature, insert the needle under the thread joining signatures one and two, then pull the thread through and into the loop that forms.

3. Enter the first sewing station of the fourth signature. Use this stitch to connect the remaining signatures.

Mock Kettle Stitch Knot

This technique uses the kettle stitch fed backwards to weave in the tail end of your thread and make a knot.

1. Thread the needle with the tail end. Run the threaded needle under the stitch adjoining the two nearest signatures.

2. Bring the needle back over this stitch, under the newly formed stitch, and then back under again. Knot.

The kettle stitch is used to join signatures in what is called a change-over stitch.

This journal is bound using the Sewn Over Tapes exposed spine binding. The covers are from a vintage textbook.

Sewn Over Tapes Exposed Spine Binding

The Sewn Over Tapes Exposed Spine binding is attractive and simple to sew. Because it has an exposed spine, the binding lies naturally flat, which is perfect for art journaling. No need to clip a book open or weight down the pages to create a flat surface. The books feel good to the hand and are a pleasure to use. You can also mix and match this technique with other stitches to add variety to your journal designs. The Sewn Over Cords Seed Pearl Stitch shown on page 20 combines well with this technique.

Materials

- book covers
- suitable paper for pages
- bone folder
- 1 to 2 yards (0.9 to 1.8 m) woven cotton or nylon fabric tape or strapping (available at fabric stores)
- awl
- large-eyed needle
- waxed linen thread (approximately 1 yard [0.9 m])
- 6 or more large binder clips
- scissors
- glue stick
- ruler
- pencil

TIPS

- Exposed-spine sewings look attractive with painted papers. This binding technique looks interesting when found papers are used for the front of each signature.

- Practice on inexpensive paper and cardboard, and save your completed practice pieces as a visual reference for various binding techniques.

- A list of helpful bookbinding books can be found in the Resources section (page 122).

MARKING THE TEMPLATE

1. Choose the material for your book covers. Using the covers from an old hardback book eliminates the need to measure and cut and offers the opportunity to recycle. The leftover text block can be cut up and used as collage material or as scrap paper for gluing.

2. Tear your paper into sheets, using your cover boards as a size guide. Each sheet should be the same height as one cover board and twice the width.

3. Fold each sheet in half widthwise to form a folio. Crease with a bone folder. Stack the folios into groups of three to five sheets to form the book's signatures. You'll need a minimum of three signatures, but the maximum is flexible.

4. Decide how many pieces of fabric tape you want to use (three is a good minimum for an average-size book) and cut them into the desired lengths. To do this, stack your signatures between the cover boards, lay the fabric tape in place, and measure the length needed for each piece of tape. Remember to extend the tape over the covers.

5. Create a sewing template with a piece of scrap paper (see page 16). Start by marking the entrance and exit holes, placing them 1/2" (1.3 cm) from either end of the template. Lay out your tapes in the space between the entrance and exit holes. Using a pencil, hold the tapes in place and mark your sewing stations on the template, adding roughly 1/8" (3 mm) to the width of each tape, to allow room for the thread to run over the tape. For example, the tapes used in the example are 1" (2.5 cm) wide, so the holes were marked 1 1/8" (2.8 cm) apart (see diagram, below).

6. Pierce the marks with the awl. Then align this template with the inside fold of each signature and push the awl through the holes, being sure to pierce through the fold of the folio at each hole.

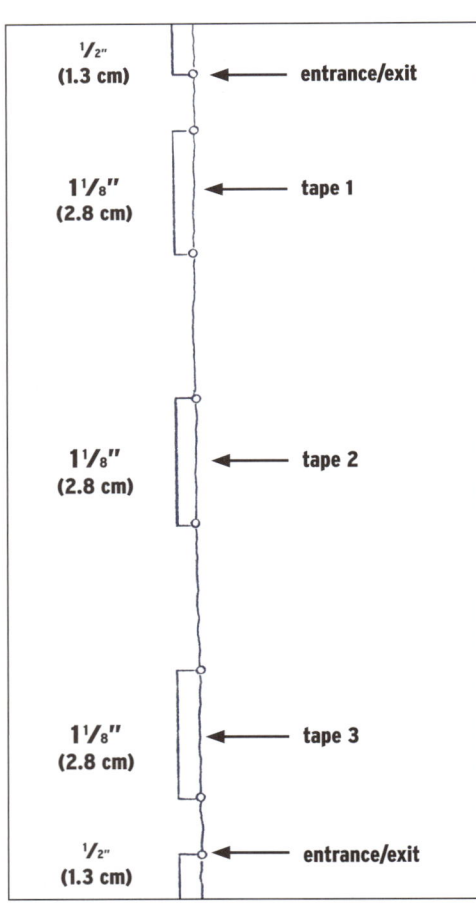

This template for piercing signatures for a Sewn Over Tapes–style journal.

Shown is the text block in progress. One signature remains to be added.

BINDING THE SIGNATURES

1. Beginning with the first signature, enter the signature with your needle and thread from the outside of the first (entrance) hole at the top of the signature. Leave a 4" (10 cm) tail of thread.

2. Come up through the next hole in the same signature. Lay your first piece of tape into place over the spine edge of the signature, carry the thread over it, and reenter the spine at the next hole. Come up through the next hole and repeat sewing over the tapes until you reach the end of the first signature's spine. Your thread should come out of the signature at the bottom (exit hole). Adjust the thread tension.

3. Enter the second signature through the bottom hole. Adjust the tension so the thread is snug but not tight. Repeat the Sewing Over Tapes process. Enter the third signature, and repeat.

4. At the end of the third signature, you will need to go back through the second and third signatures with the kettle stitch before moving on to the fourth signature. Follow the diagram and instructions on page 16.

5. Repeat this process until all the signatures have been added. Tie a square knot to tie off the thread. Return to the tail at the entrance stitch and tie it off using a mock kettle stitch knot (page 16).

ADDING THE COVERS

Lay the book covers in place over your joined signatures (text block). Using a quality glue stick or craft glue, adhere the tapes securely to the book covers. If the book is thick and the tape requires extra time to dry for maximum adherence, you might need to adhere the cover boards one at a time, clamping the tapes onto the cover with binder clips while the glue dries. When the glue has dried, repeat the process for the other cover. Often you can glue and clamp all the tapes into place, adjusting the tapes as you place each clip.

TIP

If finishing a journal and using up all the pages is important to you, make journals with fewer pages. A journal of three or four three-page signatures looks attractive but doesn't take years to fill.

This photo shows the text block completely sewn. The final step to complete the journal is to adhere the tapes to the book covers.

KETTLE STITCH BEFORE ENTERING FOURTH SIGNATURE.

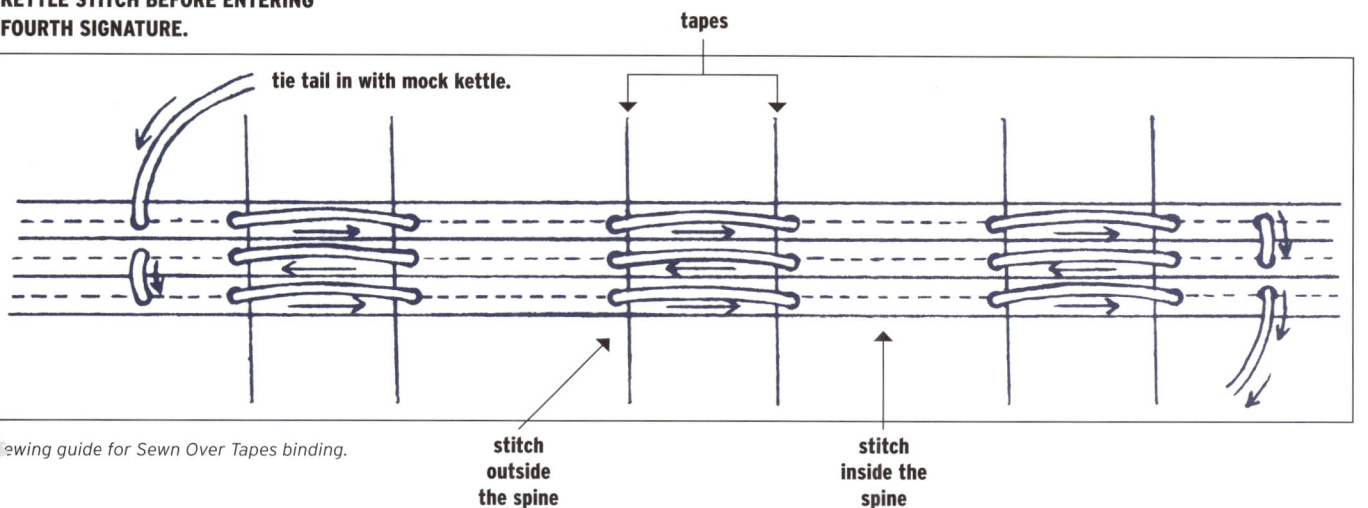

tie tail in with mock kettle.

tapes

ewing guide for Sewn Over Tapes binding.

stitch outside the spine

stitch inside the spine

Sewn Over Cords Binding with the Seed Pearl Stitch

This binding is sturdy, simple, pretty, and, like the Sewn Over Tapes binding, allows the journal to lie flat when opened for ease of use. It also allows some flexibility for cord placement on your cover boards—a plus if you're repurposing an old book and want the cover art or text to be clearly visible. You can also combine the Sewn Over Cords Seed Pearl Stitch with other exposed-spine stitches, for a variety of design options. The Sewn Over Tapes binding works wonderfully in combination with this stitch.

Keith Smith, who has produced a number of well-written books on book binding, has devoted an entire book to exposed-spine sewings. Information on Keith Smith's books can be found in the Resources section (page 122).

Materials

- optional: paper cutter
- 4 to 5 (or more) sheets of a suitable paper, sized 22" x 30" (55.5 x 76 cm)
- two cover boards
- bone folder
- ruler
- pencil
- awl
- scissors
- 1 yard (0.9 m) cotton cord or leather laces
- waxed linen thread
- needle

A Sewn Over Cords binding can be combined with other binding techniques to create a variety of designs. You can also vary the placement of the cords.

1. Tear your paper into sheets using your cover boards as a size guide. Each sheet should be the same height as one cover board and twice the width.

2. Fold each sheet in half widthwise to form a folio. Crease with a bone folder. Nest the folios into groups of three to five sheets to form the book's signatures.

3. Using a ruler and pencil, create a sewing template with entrance and exit holes and additional holes for at least two sets of cords. (You can have more than two sets of cords.) (See diagram, below.)

4. Cut two pieces of cord for each set of holes—these will become the supports for the rows of seed pearl stitches. The length of cord is determined by the width of your book. To estimate your cord length, stack your pages and sandwich them between the covers. Add a little extra—the cord can be trimmed if it's too long, but length cannot be added if it's too short.

5. Enter the first signature by pushing your needle and thread through the entrance hole from the outside of the spine. Be sure to leave a 4" to 6" (10 to 15 cm) tail.

This journal spine shows five pairs of cords and running stitches in a combination.

SEWN OVER CORDS TEMPLATE

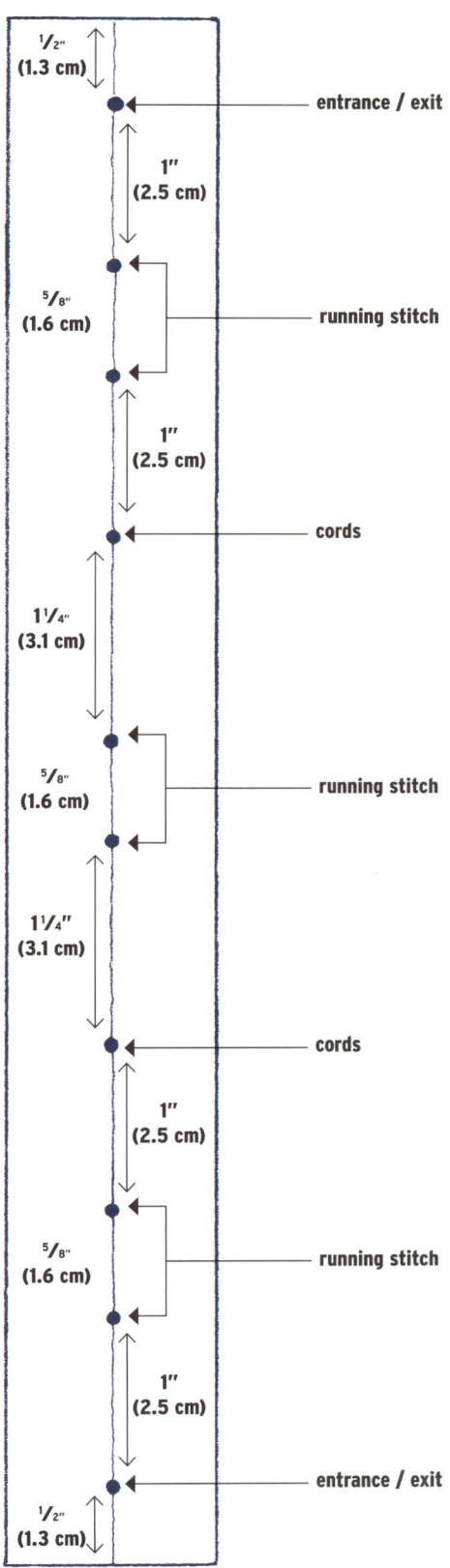

1/2" (1.3 cm)

entrance / exit

1" (2.5 cm)

running stitch

5/8" (1.6 cm)

1" (2.5 cm)

cords

1 1/4" (3.1 cm)

5/8" (1.6 cm)

running stitch

1 1/4" (3.1 cm)

cords

1" (2.5 cm)

5/8" (1.6 cm)

running stitch

1" (2.5 cm)

entrance / exit

1/2" (1.3 cm)

MAKING A SEED PEARL STITCH

1. Lay the first pair of cords over the next hole. From inside the signature, come out through the hole and between the paired cords.

2. With the needle and thread outside, wrap the thread around the two cords, moving from top to underneath. It doesn't matter in which direction you wrap.

3. After moving the thread under the two cords, bring the thread around to the top and feed the needle and thread through the loop created by the wrapping. Adjust the tension before proceeding.

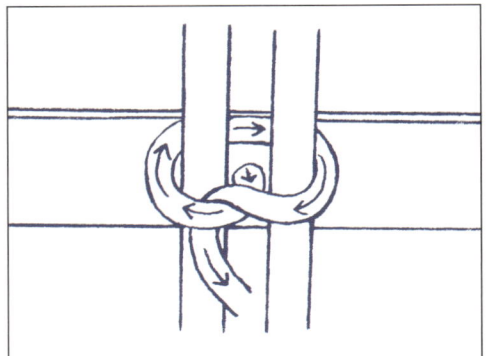

Step 1: Seed Pearl Stitch

4. Bring the thread back over the center of the loop, then insert the needle back through the original hole. Pull snug. The needle and thread will once again be on the inside of the signature.

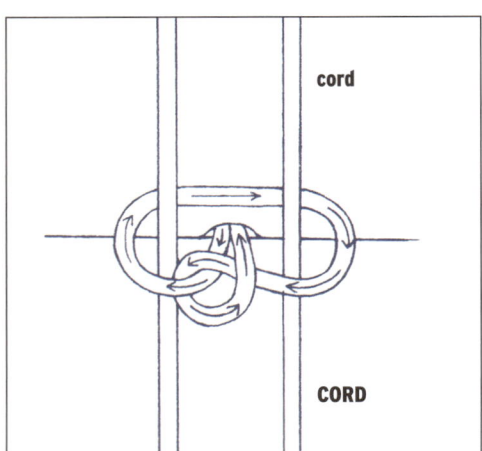

Step 2: Seed Pearl Stitch

5. Move to your next stitch. Repeat the seed pearl stitch as needed, according to your design.

6. Use the kettle stitch (page 16) to join the signatures and the mock kettle stitch knot (page 16) to work the tail into the signature.

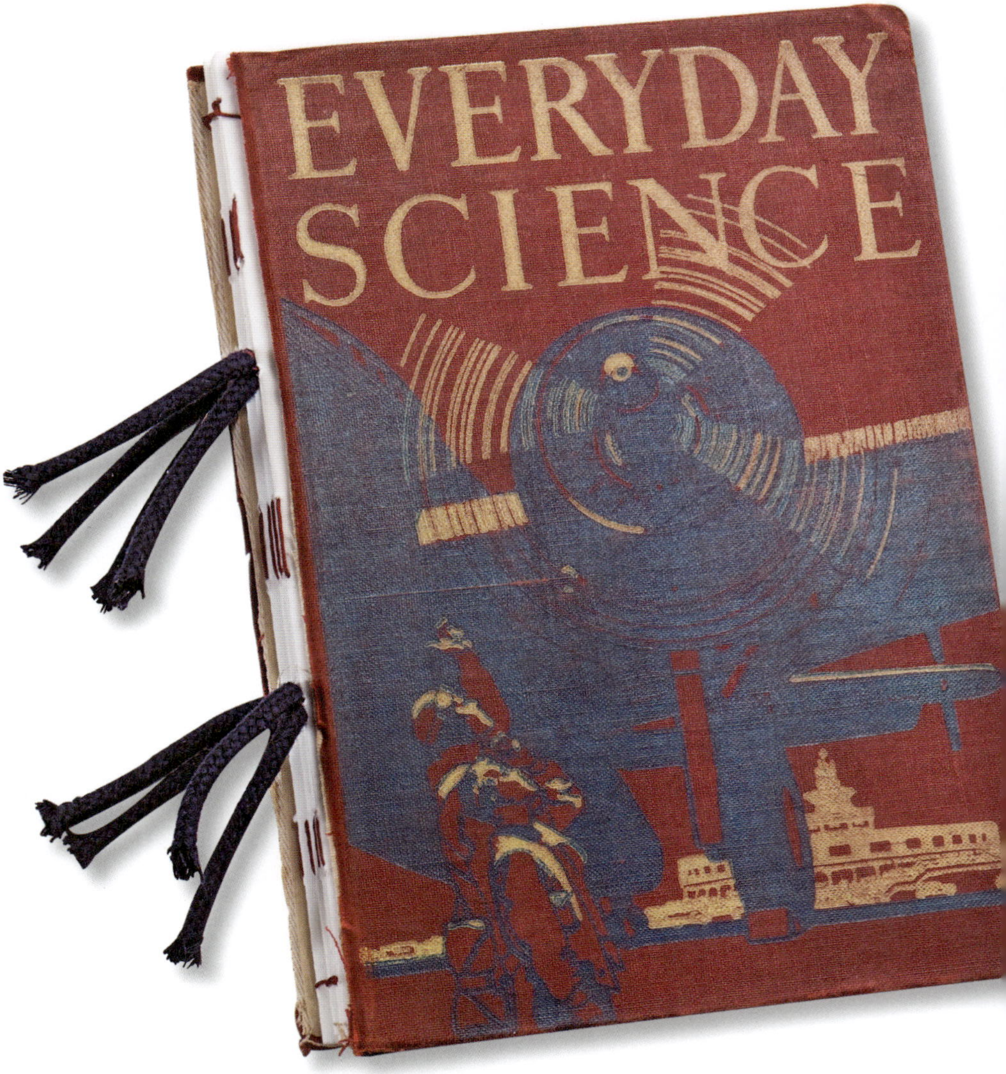

The text block of this journal is complete. Next the cover boards need to be attached.

ATTACHING THE COVER BOARDS

1. Lay your first cover board into place on the text block. With a pencil, mark the position of the cords, by placing a light mark on either side of each pair of cords. Set the text block aside.

2. Use a ruler to mark a parallel line on each side of the cord pairs. Then mark four pairs of holes for each set of parallel lines. (See the diagram, right)

3. Using an awl, pierce the holes. Lace a piece of thread through the holes, over the cords, as if lacing a shoe. Tie in a square knot inside the cover. Trim.

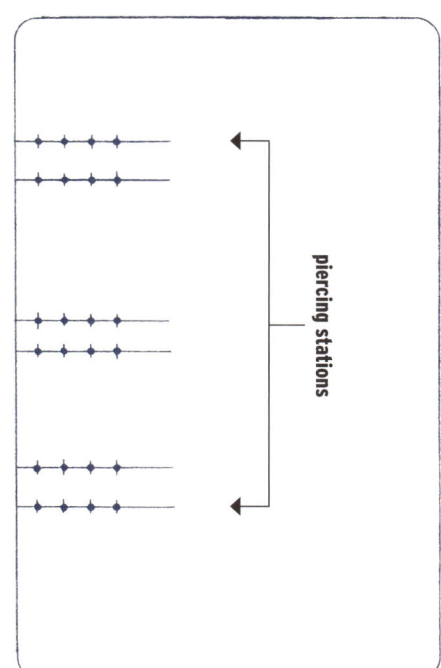

piercing stations

This template shows the piercing stations for attaching three pairs of cords to the cover boards, as shown in the journal below.

Simple Accordion-Fold Journal

This journal is easy to make, fun to work in, and has a nice fixed number of pages. These make great thematic journals that can be displayed to show the work inside.

Tina Abbott uses an accordion-fold journal to explore issues of motherhood. This style of journal is simple yet bold. Tina uses stitching, photo altering techniques, inks, and three-dimensional objects to effectively communicate her content.

Materials

- one sheet of sturdy paper, sized 22" x 30" (55.5 x 76 cm)
- bone folder
- glue
- paper trimmer or craft knife
- ruler
- two 7.5" x 11" (19 x 28 cm) pieces of heavy cardboard to use as cover boards (the covers of a discarded hardback will serve, if they're the appropriate size)

1. Fold the sheet of paper in half lengthwise; crease tightly with your bone folder. Open up the paper and repeat the fold along the same line, folding the paper the other way. Crease again. Tear along the fold line. You will have two 11" x 30" (28 x 76 cm) strips of paper.

2. Fold one strip of paper in half widthwise, then in half again, to create quarters. Each of the four sections will be approximately 11" x 7.5" (28 x 19 cm). Crease all the folds with your bone folder.

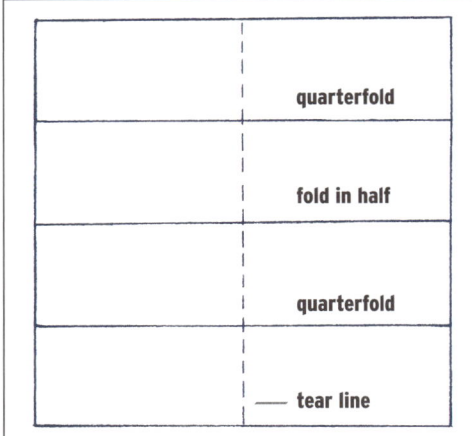

3. Repeat the folding process for the second strip. When the second strip has been folded into four equal sections, trim 5.5" (14 cm) from one end. You will have a strip with three 11" x 7.5" (28 x 19 cm) sections and one 11" x 2" (28 x 5 cm) section. You'll use this 11" x 2" (28 x 5.1 cm) section to join the two strips. (See diagram at right.)

4. Adhere the 11" x 2" (28 x 5 cm) section of the second strip to the end of your first strip, being sure to butt the edge of the first strip right up against the crease of the 2" (5.1 cm) section. The two strips combined will create one continuous sheet of folded paper with seven sections.

5. Decorate your cover boards with decorative paper or paint, or leave them as is. When the glue or paint is thoroughly dry, adhere one full section from one end of your paper strip to the back of your cover board. Allow to dry.

6. Fold all the sections closed, like an accordion, and place the book, cover side down, onto your worktable. Adhere the top section of the strip to the back of your second cover board. Allow to dry thoroughly. Your journal is ready to use.

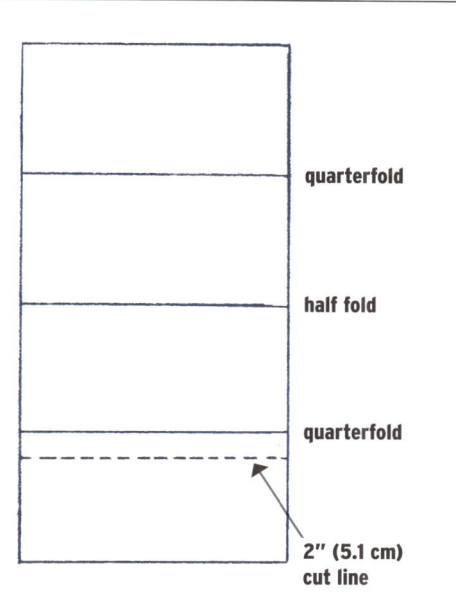

quarterfold

half fold

quarterfold

2" (5.1 cm)
cut line

TIP

When working with an accordion-fold journal, use a rubber band or ribbon tie to keep the book closed. Many art supply shops sell wide, thick rubber bands that are perfect for this use. Alternatively, skinny elastic headbands work well, come in a wide variety of colors, and are easily found in grocery, drug, department, and dollar stores.

OTHER JOURNAL STYLES

If you don't want to bind your own journal, you can adapt a purchased sketchbook or blank book by removing extra pages to create a journal with fewer pages and that allows room for the expansion that naturally occurs from collaging materials onto the pages. Be sure to choose a sketchbook or blank book with sewn-in folios and sturdy paper.

If you have chosen a journal with light-weight paper and find that it is not suitable for some of the mediums you want to try, you can increase the sturdiness of your pages by gluing several together. Glue them together by adding one page at a time, and allow them to dry before gluing additional pages. The most effective way of doing this is to apply glue to the entire right-hand sheet of a pair of pages. Place a piece of waxed paper under the page to catch excess glue. Flip the left-hand page onto theright-hand page and smooth down the pages. Carefully drag an old credit card or razor

blade over the pages to remove the air bubbles. Allow the pages to dry thoroughly—wet paper is fragile. You can also add a coat of gesso to your pages to create a surface on which you can use paint more easily. Other journal options are attractive ring binders and scrapbooks, which you can find in the scrapbooking section of craft shops. Filled with your own papers, the binders make wonderful journals. A plus is that you can work on a single sheet at a time without worrying about messing up or splattering the other pages.

You can also create a journal from single-sheet work by housing the sheets in a portfolio. Archival boxes are available from photography suppliers, but you can make a simple envelope-style portfolio yourself using canvas and a sewing machine.

Karen Cole uses the handmade portfolio option to great effect (see page 11). First, determine your page size. Cut a piece of canvas 3" to 5" (7.6 to 12.7 cm) longer than your pages are wide and 2" (5.1 cm) wider than the pages are long. Fold the piece of canvas, with the longer side held vertically

nearly in half, leaving a 3" to 5" (7.6 to 12.7 cm) flap. Machines stitch the sides with a 1/2" (1.3 cm) seam allowance.

The book continues as an artistic form to evolve and artists continually test the parameters of what constitutes a book. Don't be afraid to create a journal that is outside the covers of a book if that is what suits your style or needs best.

TIP

Give a purchased journal a vintage feel by adhering a slightly smaller vintage book cover to the front. You can convert an old coffee table book into a journal without rebinding it by coating the pages with gesso and gluing pages together (as described at left).

This purchased sketchbook has been personalized by painting on the cover. First, the rectangle was masked off, using masking tape. A coat of gesso was applied and allowed to dry. Acrylic paints were layered and reductive stenciling (page 37) was used.

KEEPER OF THE FLAME:

AN INTERVIEW WITH BRENDA BEENE SHACKLEFORD

Brenda Beene Shackleford is an artist and graphic designer who is a longtime art journaler with a strong commitment to involving others in the practice of art journaling.

Can you describe your internal process for journaling?

Most of the time, when I'm journaling, I do it to remember things, the way my life is now. For the visual journals, I don't think too much when I'm working in them. The pages have no agenda, other than letting my mind play and let loose, which is a tough thing for a graphic designer to do. When I'm designing for a client, everything on the page is planned and has a place and purpose. My art pages are more about what I'm feeling at the time I create them; they're more intuitive, not so much a planned layout. I'm working toward being more introspective and digging deeper into my thoughts and feelings surrounding my life. Journaling has been a great tool in helping me through some emotional rough patches that life has thrown at me along the way. It's helpful and healing to be able to put feelings into words and pictures.

Do you have a number of journals going at once?

Not really. I have lot of half-started, partially prepped journals that are just sitting blank, languishing from lack of attention. I usually create in spurts. For the past eight or nine years, I've been keeping an "everyday" journal. It's a small Moleskine that I carry with me everywhere.

What advice would you give a beginner regarding content?

Do what interests you—don't worry about what everyone else is doing or about the hot theme that's showing up in all the art magazines. It's fine if it's something that brings you joy, but don't use an image or style of collage just because it's popular with the masses. The quality of your art will show through if it's truly from the heart. When you create something you love or that holds interest for you, it speaks to others.

Where do you work on your art journals?

Mainly, I work on my journals at home in my newly acquired studio. But if it's a travel journal, I like to work on-site as much as possible. Before I leave on my trip, I usually prep some of the pages with imagery or color that coordinates with the destination. I'll add photos from the trip later.

Brenda Beene Shackleford created this journal page by using painting to extend the image, shown on the right page, across the entire spread.

Using rich color and dramatic paint strokes, this journal page spread vibrates with emotional content.

Brenda keeps journals of her travels and adventures, using purchased journals, pen and ink drawings, and watercolor.

CHAPTER 2:
THE TINDERBOX: PAGE SURFACE TECHNIQUES

Think of your blank journal as a tinderbox, a box for holding combustible materials, ready to catch fire when you sit down to work. Your journal can be an exciting place to explore and visit—definitely a potentially explosive place! Journal pages can explode with creativity, with physical manifestations of our experiences and ideas. It is far better to face the page with excitement than with the fear of making a mistake!

As the song says: "Begin at the very beginning; it is a very good place to start." The first step is to apply *something* to the blank page—paint, ink, paper—to add visual content to the page surface. Dozens of techniques and mediums can be used to apply a surface layer to your journal pages. In this chapter, we'll ignite your creativity with a sampling of techniques using acrylic paints, gesso, ink, and paper, as well as watercolors, watercolor crayons, pastels, and water-soluble oil crayons, to create interesting surfaces for your journal pages.

If you like to bind your own journals, you can apply many of these technique to your pages before binding, so you have prepped pages in your journal. You can work with full or partial sheets of paper you haven't yet made to folio size, or work on each folio separately. Remember to work on both sides of the paper.

This journal page was first coated with gesso and then followed by layers of acrylic paint. Some of the top layers were removed by scrubbing.

Painted with acrylics and worked using abstract ovoid shapes, the artist, Tina Abbott created a page surface that she opted to leave stand on its own.

ACRYLIC PAINT PAGE SURFACES

Scraped Paint

Acrylic paints are a great way to add bold, rich, varied color to journal pages. Unfortunately, when applied using most painting techniques, the acrylic paint will adhere to the adjoining page once the pages of the journal are closed. Prying them apart typically ruins the art on both pages. However, if applied thinly enough, acrylic paints can be used on page surfaces. The trick is to use just enough paint to add color, but not enough to make the page sticky or tacky. The method that follows is wonderfully simple and can be used to create pages with interesting visual texture. Acrylic paint can be scraped along the paper surface with an old plastic credit card forcing the paint into the porous surface of the paper. The excess paint is scraped away, and a rich, pigmented, nonsticky surface remains.

Materials

- newspaper
- bucket of water
- covering for work surface
- apron
- sturdy paper
- acrylic paints
- old plastic cards (credit cards, reward cards, gift cards, hotel key cards)
- spray bottle with water
- paper towels

1. Cover your work surface and put on an apron or smock. Tip: a stack of old newspapers provides an excellent work surface; the newspaper pages can be discarded as paint builds up.

2. Tear your paper down to the desired size.

3. Lay out your papers and assemble your paints.

4. Squeeze out a thick line of paint from the tube along one edge of your first piece of paper. Holding a plastic card at an angle, scrape the paint firmly across the paper from one edge to the other.

You will have paint building up on your plastic card; this is okay. Continue to scrape the paint across the paper. You will be able to see where paint is laying on the paper more thickly in comparison to scraped areas. Scraped areas will look smoother and not as shiny and wet as thicker areas. Thicker areas become sticky areas. It will seem as though you are embedding the pigment of the paint into the paper.

You may find that the paint will bleed under the edges of your painter paper slightly, or you will slip when scraping and get paint on the reverse. Don't worry—this creates more visual texture. When you are done with the first side, flip the paper over and scrape any thick paint, or wipe it with a baby wipe. You won't remove that paint, but you will work it into the surface. It is best to work both sides of the paper in the same color families.

Using the scraped paint technique, the artist created a journal of colors that spoke of winter. White acrylic paint was laid down first. Other colors were subsequently applied to create a muted winter palette.

The paint build up on your cards can be used on the reverse side of your paper or on another page. If you are finished with that color, wipe the excess onto a paper towel. Drop the plastic card into your bucket of water.

Important: You should work quickly to avoid adhering the paper to your work surface.

You can apply a second and third layer to create wonderful effects. Simply repeat the steps above. When applying a third layer, you will get better results if the second layer has gone from being wet to being tacky to the touch. You don't need to cover the first layer of paint entirely.

At this point, you have two options:

Add a second paint color. You can apply it over the whole surface or just in certain sections.

Using a spray bottle, mist the still-wet surface with water. Misting will produce small droplets of water; to create larger droplets, place your fingertip over the hole in the nozzle of the spray bottle. Wait several seconds, then lay a roll of paper towels at one edge of the page. Unroll it across your paper, pressing as you go, then lift off the paper towel. This technique creates interesting visual texture and reveals through the droplets the surface under the most recent layer of paint. You can add a second color before misting or mist after applying each layer of paint. Avoid mixing too many colors; which can result in a muddy, dull surface.

VARIATIONS

A spray bottle of water and paper towels can be used to create an interesting pattern with two or more layers of paint. Where the water droplets have fallen, the paint can be removed and creates great additional texture while showing revealing both paint layers.

1. Using a spray bottle, mist the still-tacky surface with water. Misting will produce smaller droplets and a smaller, tighter pattern. To create larger droplets and a looser pattern, place your fingertip over the hole in the nozzle of the spray bottle while you spray the paper.

2. Wait several (10 to 15) seconds and then unroll some paper towels and lay them on the surface. Press down on the towels, blotting up the water. The first layer of paint will be revealed where ever the paint is lifted.

You can add a third color of paint and repeat the technique. Avoid too many layers as they can result in muddy colors and stickiness.

TIP

If you bind your own journals, painting your pages before binding them is a great way to make a journal of pages that are ready to receive collage, additional painting with water-soluble crayons, photographs, image transfers, or drawing with colored pencils, permanent markers, or gel pens.

Acrylic paint can also be scraped over existing work in a journal to create another layer, obscure text, or rework a journal page with which you are not satisfied.

TIP

To fix a page that you don't like, allow it to dry completely. Then, choosing a darker paint color, scrape the paint over the surface. Use the spray bottle technique described above and mist the surface. You can also apply the darker paint color, and use the Reductive Stenciling technique on page 37, instead of the spray bottle technique.

Scraped paint surfaces fill this book. They were applied prior to binding.

VARIATIONS

Use rubber stamps to add or remove color. To add color, apply acrylic paint to the stamp surface with a foam cosmetic sponge and stamp onto your surface. To remove color, apply the rubber stamp to the wet paint surface and remove; the stamp will blot off some of the paint.

Use gel medium and foam stamps to create a patterned texture. Apply gel medium to a foam stamp with a cosmetic sponge and stamp on the painted page surface. Allow the gel medium to dry. Apply a second color of paint, then use a damp cloth to gently wipe away some of the paint from the stamped surface. The dried gel medium acts as a resist and reveals the color beneath.

This pair of journal pages use scraped paint, reductive stenciling, and stenciling with gesso as a base. Collage was used on top of the paint, creating a surface for journaling.

Painter's tape was used to create a ragged border around the edge of these pages.

This journal page was created by adhering various papers to the page surface and then wiping some acrylic paint on the surface. A bit of stenciling with gesso decorates the right side.

FIRE STARTER:

Masking

Use masking tape (or painter's tape for more fragile paper surfaces) to mask off areas before painting. You can also add tape in midprocess. Just be sure the paint is completely dry before you apply the tape. Using masking tape is a creative way to frame pages, and the taped-off areas provide wonderful places to add text. Masking tape can be found in widths as narrow as 1/8" (3 mm).

Try making masks in various shapes from low-tack shelf paper or cardstock. If using cardstock, coat the reverse side of the finished mask with low-tack or repositionable spray adhesive. This helps seal the mask to the paper so that paint does not leak under the edges.

Avoiding the Blank Page

The biggest advantage of applying materials to your pages before you sit down to journal is that you have a book of surfaces that allow you to escape the whole "blank page" syndrome—the not-so-amusing phenomenon of opening your art journal to a blank page and suddenly losing every creative thought you had. I almost always have a journal of surfaces ready to go. Then, if I have a day of blank mind, or monkey mind (you know, where you have more ideas than common sense and can't settle on a place to begin), I have pages that have already been started. I choose a page or page spread with colors that connect to an image I want to use or thought I am having, and, before long, I'm on to the next journal page.

The left side of the journal illustrates simple reductive stenciling. This journal is small–3.5" x 5" –and the simple number stencil offers big impact and good contrast to the drawn and painted image on the right.

REDUCTIVE STENCILING

Stenciling is an interesting way to apply texture and pattern to paper. One method of stenciling on a journal page without creating a buildup of paint and causing pages to stick together is reductive stenciling. In reductive stenciling, instead of applying paint through the stencil openings, paint is removed from the stencil openings.

Materials

- covering for work surface
- apron
- sturdy paper
- acrylic paints
- plastic cards
- plastic stencils
- damp rag or baby wipes
- spray bottle of water
- paper towels

1. Use the Scraped Paint technique described on page 32.

2. While the top layer of paint is wet, or at least tacky to the touch, place a plastic stencil onto your painted page surface.

3. Using a damp rag or baby wipe, remove the paint through the openings of the stencil until you are satisfied with the appearance.

4. You may wish to reposition your stencil, working in different areas of your page. You may also opt to remove paint from around the outside edge of the stencil to create a bordered effect.

5. You can create shaded effects by removing paint in varying amounts and change the look of a stenciled pattern by only removing paint through some of the stencil openings.

6. You can also use a spray bottle filled with water and paper towels to use the technique described on page 33 to add another layer of visual texture. Alternately, you can use this same technique before using the stencil.

7. You can also use multiple stencils with an additional layer or two of paint. Be sure to allow the first stenciled layer to dry completely before adding on the next layer of paint to keep the design shapes more recognizable and prevent the muddying of the colors. The additional paint layers should be applied using the Scraped Paint technique (see page 32). Keep in mind that adding more layers of paint and reductive stenciling will alter and obscure the first stencil design somewhat.

FIRE STARTER:

Simple Stencils

- Punchinella, the waste strip left from sequin production, makes wonderful stencils. The size of circular patterns vary with the size of the sequins. Punchinella can be purchased online or in craft shops.

- Plastic lace place mats and sections of plastic lace tablecloths make pretty stencils. Crocheted doilies also make lovely lace stencils.

- Plastic-mesh produce bags can make loose background stencils.

- Simple silhouette stencils can be cut from magazine covers or heavy magazine pages. Use the negative image as the stencil, by removing the paint from within the silhouette. Use the positive image as a mask, by removing paint from around the paper silhouette.

- Mesh drywall tape, found at the hardware store, makes a great stencil.

WORKING WITH GESSO

Gesso is useful for creating page surfaces and manipulating page content. Experiment with colored gesso, too, which can be used in any of the ways described for acrylic paints.

Gesso Sgraffito

Sgraffito is a technique in which a layer of color is scratched to reveal the layer beneath. The term comes from the Italian word *sgraffire*, which means "to scratch." For this technique, apply gesso in large swaths or small areas over a page painted with acrylics. While the gesso is still *wet*, use a skewer or other tool to scratch into the gesso to create interesting textures. Dry gesso is riskier to scratch into, because you can easily tear through the page. If you want to give the dry gesso sgraffito technique a try, scratch with a tool similar to a straightened paper clip.

Brenda Shackleford uses gesso to create excellent emotional effect on this page.

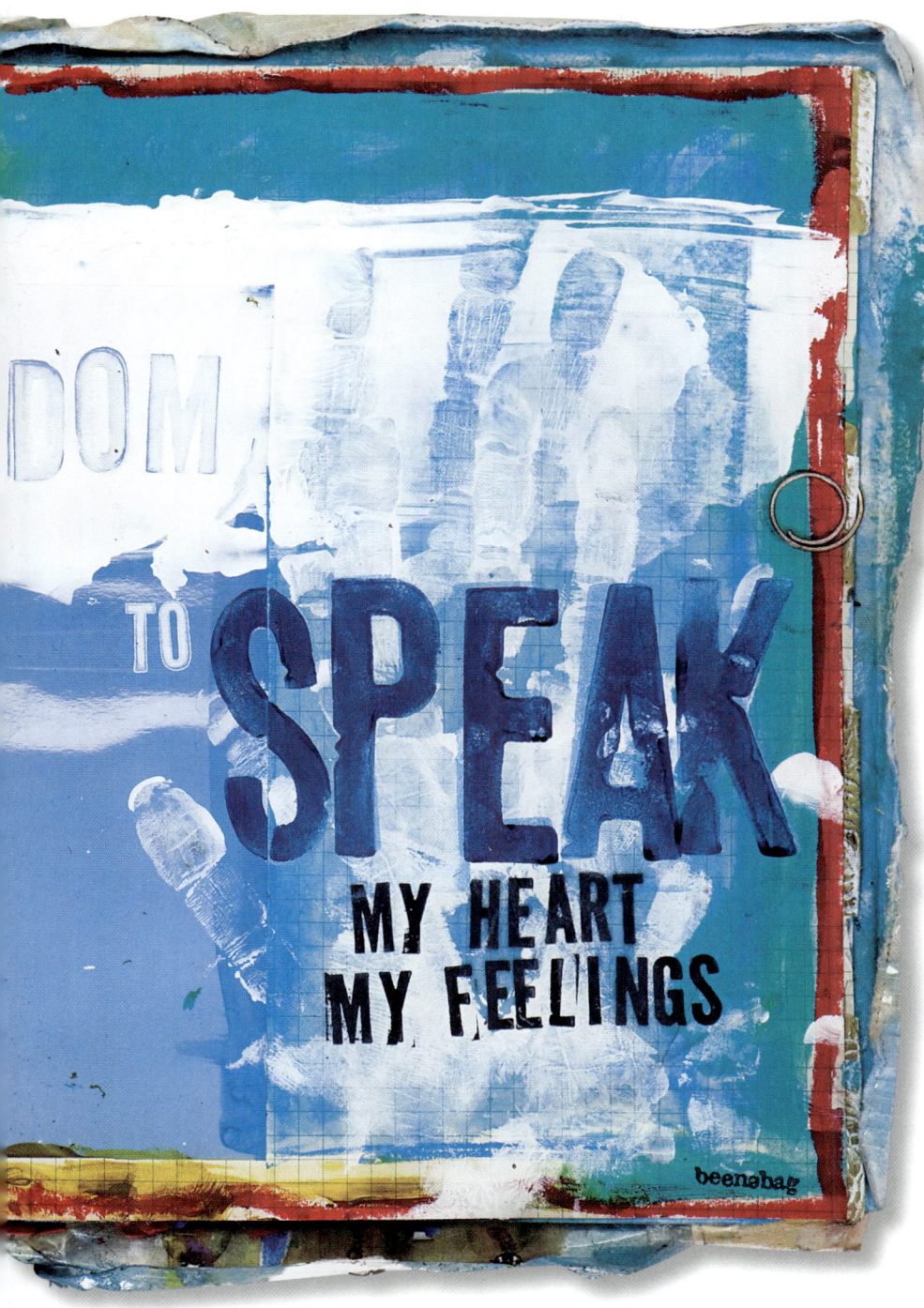

Combed Gesso

Wet gesso can be manipulated with rubber combing tools. The result is similar to the look of paste paper. You can use purchased colored gesso or gesso you've tinted yourself for this technique. Rubber combing tools are available at craft shops, art suppliers, and hardware stores in the faux-finish paint sections.

Materials

- paper surface
- gesso
- rubber combing tools, hair comb, notched plastic cards
- wide paintbrush
- paint

1. Begin with either a painted or unpainted surface. Working quickly, apply gesso across your page. You can coat the entire page or apply a rough coat, leaving bare patches.

2. Drag your combing tool across the wet gesso; the tool will create lines. Feel free to play: make waves, circles, cross-hatching lines, or any pattern you like. The tool exposes the layer below and provides visual and physical texture.

3. Allow the gesso to dry completely. If you like, apply a layer of paint over the page with a wide brush, and then wipe the paint off, to leave the raised design. Or, if your background was painted before you applied the gesso, you can simply begin to work on the journal page.

Gesso and Paint Stenciling

This technique uses stencils in the traditional way, but applying a mixture of gesso and paint through the stencil openings decreases the potential for pages ticking together.

This journal was constructed using 4" x 5" (10.2 x 12.7 cm) sheets of mat board. Each board was covered on both sides with papers that had been painted with acrylic and stenciling that was applied using both gesso and paint and reductive stenciling methods.

Materials

- foam tray or plate
- acrylic paint
- gesso
- stencil adhesive or repositionable adhesive
- plain printer paper
- journal pages
- paper towels
- stencil
- stencil brushes

1. On a plate or tray, mix small amounts of acrylic paint and gesso.

2. Spray the reverse side of your stencil with stencil adhesive or repositionable adhesive. Use a very light hand to avoid creating thick, sticky blobs. If you have overapplied the spray, blot it off with a piece of plain printer paper. Lay the stencil in the desired position on your journal page.

3. Dip a clean, dry stencil brush into the gesso-and-paint mixture. On a paper towel, work the stencil brush to remove most of the paint from the brush.

4. Pounce the brush, using an up-and-down movement, into the stencil openings. Start at the center of the stencil opening and work out to the edges.

5. When the stencil pattern is completely painted, carefully remove the stencil.

6. If necessary, place a clean sheet of printer paper onto the stenciled pattern. Smooth gently to blot any excess paint.

PAPER SURFACES

Various papers can be used to create a starting surface for journaling. You can simply cover a page with a piece of decorative paper or ephemera and add layers from there, but you can also use papers to apply texture, image, and color to a page. Excellent papers to use for this technique include phone book pages, newspapers, paper bags, tissue papers, junk mail, catalog pages, and pieces torn from magazines. Using a variety of different papers on a single page can seem as though it might detract from the cohesiveness of a page, but actually, multiple papers can create visual texture and increase the energy of page (and, it is a lot of fun!)

You can add cohesiveness with the next layer a number of ways: by applying a thin layer of paint, using a stencil, or making use of the paper as a background on which to draw or to transfer a photograph.

By covering her journal pages in a variety of surfaces before journaling and collaging further, Mary Ann Moss creates a rich textural surface over which she's used spray paint and masking.

Materials

- paper scraps
- adhesive (gel medium works well)
- journal pages
- paintbrushes

1. To create the initial page surface—one step up from a blank page—select some papers and tear them into strips or small pieces.

2. Using your adhesive, adhere the paper pieces to your page in a way that pleases you, remembering that other layers, such as paint, images, drawing, or writing, will be applied over these paper pieces. Wrinkles can be visually interesting, too, so work freely, and don't worry about laying them down perfectly.

3. When the papers have dried completely, you can apply a layer of paint using any of the described acrylic paint techniques or doodle or mark onto the surface with water-soluble crayons, colored pencils, china markers, or other mediums. This is an ideal time to begin adding imagery, such as collage elements, photographs, prints, or drawings.

Using layers of found images, paint, papers, photos, and text with deftly chosen colors, Mary Ann creates complex journal pages without creating heaviness.

Reclamation: A Scrap Paper Journal

Junk mail, postcard advertisements, and catalogs are terrific sources of paper. Consider using these as paper pages in themselves. Yes, make a journal from junk mail or a catalog! Use junk mail and heavier catalog pages as the paper for your pages, or create a small journal from binder rings and the postcard advertisements that find their way into your mailbox. The idea of repurposing these materials to create a journal page or an entire journal is exciting.

Artist Pam Garrison used a catalog from a gardening store and pieces of decorative paper, vintage wallpaper, and other ephemera from her studio to create a fabulous journal to take with her when she traveled to artfiberfest, an annual fabric arts retreat. Pam covered each section of the accordion-fold style catalog with various papers and inspirational images. Each section varies slightly from its neighboring section. Continuity is created by choosing papers whose colors fall within a chosen color palette. Florals dominate as a design element and also help tie the pages together.

The original catalog that Pam Garrison repurposed into a journal

Pam Garrison's finished tri-fold journal

Wonder

play

By Frida Wolfe

see

Joan Garrison

FINIS

SUMMER'S SWEET SORBETS

DO

ART FIBER FEST

page

6

renting a car
Sat. night @ the airport
worked out great.

Bread & Ink
735th & Hawthorne
508-281-7694
9:30 am Sunday
lunch w/ Sheila
+ Denise
then to ↓

Flutter
A DELIGHTFUL DISARRAY OF
FOUND OBJECTS AND CLUTTER
3948 N. MISSISSIPPI AVE.
PORTLAND, OR 97227
P. 503.288.1649
flutterclutter.com

CRAFTY
WONDERLAND
40 VENDORS SELLING AMAZING HANDMADE GOODS

Travel =
sometimes

TO
MOM
Love,
Dagie

This scrap paper journal by L. K. Ludwig was created using two quadfold exterior paint brochures, two pieces of mat board, and the Sewn Over Cords Binding technique shown on page 20.

Inspired by Pam and a trip to the hardware store, I discovered that the large tri- and quad-fold paint sample brochures have a great sturdy surface. I used three of these folded brochures to create a fun journal.

Materials

- gesso

- paintbrush

- three or more large folded brochures on heavy stock

- binding supplies (choose a binding technique of your liking: the sample uses the Sewn Over Cords technique, page 20; the Sewn Over Tapes technique, page 17, also works well)

- two pieces of mat board or cardboard the size of a folded brochure

1. Apply a light coat of gesso to all the brochure surfaces and allow it to dry completely.

2. Decide on assembly. If you have a quadfold brochure, use each folded brochure as both your folio and signature. (The folded brochure is too thick to stack multiple folios in a single signature.) For a trifold brochure, you will need to choose which crease to use as the center of your folio. The third flap just folds over, so that one side of your folio is a single sheet, and the other side is a foldout of two sheets. Choose your binding technique and follow the instructions with each brochure as a signature.

3. Attach the cover boards as required by your binding. Paint or cover them with decorative paper before binding, if desired.

Here, L. K.'s scrap paper journal, made using three quad-folded paint brochures, is shown with one of the quad-folded brochures opened completely. Both ends fold in to the center, so each brochure provides eight segments, including front and back.

KEEPER OF THE FLAME:
INSIGHTS FROM KATIE KENDRICK

Katie Kendrick is an amazing artist and an excellent workshop instructor whose painting style is rich with emotional content and whose journal pages are thick with layers of work. Her authenticity is both inspiring and reassuring. I asked Katie to share her internal work process.

COMMITMENT TO THE PROCESS AND THE PRACTICE OF MAKING ART

My studio is in the house. When we had the house built, I called the two-car garage space my workspace. Just being in the studio, setting foot in there, is my cue to create. It's something I look forward to doing with a passion. To give up an entire day to something else, like cleaning, laundry, cooking, and other household jobs . . . no, I rarely do that! I work those activities around my studio time.

When I first started out, I read something Teesha Moore wrote: "If you want to be an artist, all you have to do is put in the time." That was a mind-bending breakthrough for me—I didn't have to be good; all I had to do was do it! She suggested twenty minutes a day, which seemed totally doable. So I established that habit—twenty minutes minimum per day on most days. More often than not, I would work much longer, because it took twenty minutes of priming to get me in the flow, and, once there, I didn't want to leave.

I'm not a superdisciplined person, so if I didn't have the passion for creating that I do, I just wouldn't put in the time. It's a bit like having a love affair, being swept off my feet, not caring about anything but the process of creating; it can be so passionate—most of the time, anyway. Art is the door that takes me to that most alive place.

Katie Kendrick's journal is housed between covers removed from an old atlas. Fabric forms the spine to which the pages are sewn.

These page from Katie Kendrick's journal were created on a variety of reclaimed and repurposed papers, including grocery bags.

DOING THE WORK

First thing in the morning, I'll tidy up my workspace if I've worked late the day or night before and left it a mess. I like the calm of blank paper and fresh water to start. I work on several pieces at once and go back and forth. I have large, loose journal pages, small postcard-size pages that will go into a book one day, canvases, sewing projects . . . I'll just start where I feel the impulse to start. I store the projects-in-process in bins, so I can put them in unfinished and bring them out again when the urge strikes me. I work best when I can work on several things in several stages. It might seem scattered, but I feel most comfortable working this way. I don't count on starting and finishing a piece in one day, although that does happen; it doesn't bother me at all to leave things unfinished indefinitely. I'm interested in being in the process, in the creative state.

About the way I work: In the beginning, paint felt threatening, and I had the misconception that I couldn't paint, so I didn't want to try. I imagined I would feel worse trying and having it look awful than not trying at all. What I didn't realize, until I started painting, was how enjoyable the process is, and, once I started, I was hooked. I began to realize that, when I stepped aside and just got lost in the act of moving paint around, gluing, cutting, tearing, I had this timeless feeling, and hours would pass without me knowing where it had gone. When I felt sad, I noticed that my paintings would reflect that somehow; when I was angry or agitated, I noticed that I moved my brush differently, that I was more forceful and my work reflected my emotion, even though I didn't consciously try to impact the piece.

Many times, I will put together images that don't appear to have any conscious meaning for me, and only later will I see why it resonated with some part of me or with some event that was taking place in my life. Once I realized that, when I step back, paintings and journal pages really create themselves, I became an enthralled observer as well as a participant. I noticed that questions would arise as I worked—the "what if I did that" kind of questions—and I started to follow them. I became aware that I was a happier person, now that I was doing my art with a passion, that it spilled over into all areas of my life. It helped balance my moods and provide me with an outlet for them. My journal is my mirror to my subconscious; it tells me things that I don't think I know about myself. And it's fun—just one gigantic experiment that I get to repeat in every way I can imagine. What can be better than that?

I think the biggest gift I can give my students is to embody the process of letting go and model intuitive art making. I remind them that the process is where the juiciness is, where the life is, that when they have a finished piece, that particular journey is over, so enjoy the moments of creating.

Combining painting, drawing, collage, photography, and writing, Katie's journals are complex views of experiences, thoughts, imagining, and creations.

Each page in this large journal is sewn to a
side of a fabric strip, which forms a folio.
Each folio is then sewn into the book,
forming the book structure.

CHAPTER 3:

BUILDING A FIRE: USING IMAGERY

There are a number of ways an artist can communicate information on an art journal page—color, texture, and line can all work to convey information and emotion. However, the most direct way of communicating content on an art journal page is to use imagery. The process of adding images on journal pages, whether the image is a manipulated photograph, a pen-and-ink sketch, or scrap paper collage allows you, the artist, to provide form to what you have in mind to say on your pages.

Rich compositions can be created using images that are readily available. Journals, by and large, are for personal use, which allows the artist to work with images found in magazines and books. Digital photography has made journal pages affordable and accessible. Collage elements are everywhere, arriving in junk mail, blowing along the sidewalk, or awaiting purchase at art supply or scrapbooking stores.

When you continue to work with an image you have found or created by changing it in some way— adding to it with drawing, altering it with collage, or enhancing it in some other way—you add meaning to the image because you have added content to the image. As a consequence, your journal page becomes more personal and authentic, and you are able to thoroughly experience what the art journaling process offers.

Jan Harris uses painting and drawing to create journal pages that are rich in imagery. She makes use of watercolor, acrylic, gouache, and pen and ink in her journals.

U-CUT FLOWERS
2/25¢ Sunflowers.5¢

RASMUSSEN FARMS
HOOD RIVER, OR
"VAN GOGH DAYS"
8/6/06

THE SIGHT OF THE STARS MAKES ME DREAM, WITH ANY CERTAINTY BUT FOR MY PART I KNOW NOTHING WITH WINGS. (BLAKE). FOR HE SOARS WITH HIS OWN TOO HIGH, IF HE SOARS WITH HIS OWN FLY AWAY. NO BIRD SOARS

VAN GOGH

ADDING IMAGERY THROUGH COLLAGE

A collage is defined as an artistic composition of materials and objects pasted over a surface, often with unifying lines and color. This broad definition underscores why collage is one of the most commonly used techniques on an art journal page—there is an enormous amount of flexibility and possibility in collage.

Collage requires only scissors, paper, and adhesive. Paper for use in collage is all over your house. From telephone books, newspapers, magazines, and junk mail, to coffee filters, paper towels, and gift tissue, materials that you can use in a paper collage on a journal page abound. Not only is it an inexpensive way to work in your journal, it allows you to repurpose stuff that might otherwise get thrown away or placed in a recycling bin. A variety of adhesives are available to use in paper collage. A simple glue stick will do the job. Visit your local craft store and read labels on the various adhesives, looking for one that is specifically for paper so that wrinkling is minimal; common types of adhesives for collage include spray adhesives, pastes, and gel mediums. This definition is fairly broad and underscores why collage is one of the most commonly used art journaling techniques—there is an enormous amount of flexibility and possibility in collage.

You can use several approaches to collage in your art journal. One easy way to use collage in your journal is to create a beginning page surface as a jumping-off point for your journal page. To do this, apply pieces of found paper in either a random or deliberate pattern. Pieces of paper taken from the newspaper or phone book make great background textures and lines without adding meaning. Then, apply a thin coat of gesso across the surface obscuring most of the text. From there, you can draw, paint, add more collage, include a photo, or any combination of techniques. Another way to work with collage in your journal is to use it abstractly to create a mood, by choosing a particular color, cutting or tearing your papers into specific shapes, and creating a line that the eye can follow using pieces of paper. Collage can also be used to create a border around a drawing, a painting, or a photograph. This border can emphasize the image, or can integrate the image into the page—all depending on the colors of the papers, their shapes, and whether or not you add paint or marks.

Blocks of color, wrinkled or textured papers, and papers with text or pattern can all be used to create interesting effects. The papers you choose for collage can influence the overall content of your art journal page. A collage of vintage papers and ephemera can create a sense of history and communicate points in time or nostalgic feelings about the past.

Collage can also be used to illustrate people and things, à la Eric Carle (children's book author and illustrator) who cuts and layers his hand-painted papers to illustrate various characters and creatures in his books. By cutting up your own photos, images from magazines, or colored scraps of paper, you can recombine them to create entirely new images of people, animals, and locations. In this way, you have created your own original images to communicate visually on your journal pages.

Collage is a great way to ignite an art journal page for beginners or anyone suffering from creative block or as an everyday practice to get you moving on your art journaling wildfire. With its minimal supply requirements and scrap paper available everywhere you go, collage is also perfect for on-the-go journaling.

Judi Delgado uses collage techniques to create page surfaces and page content as part of her journaling process. Often creating layers with torn papers—strips or rectangles—to create line and movement on her pages, Judi adds image and text on top.

come back feeling different.

when she hesitated to speak
should remember much that

Using layers of transparent rice paper, pieces of book pages, photographs, and trim, Brenda Shackleford created a journal page spread that flows from left to right as the viewer's eye is drawn across the page.

Strips of paper are combined with collaged photos and image transfers for a haunting effect in this journal page by Judi Delgado.

Simple Paper Collage

A simple way to use collage, if you are new to the medium, is to create a background of simple shapes and texture for your journal page.

Materials

- old phone book or magazines
- journal
- adhesive
- gesso
- 2" to 3" (5 to 7.5 cm) paintbrush
- acrylic paint

1. Tear directory pages from the phone book or advertisement pages from a magazine. Tear the pages into mostly rectangular shapes.

2. Adhere the pieces to your journal page in a pleasing way. One easy and interesting way to begin is to make a grid of shapes, three columns wide.

3. After your papers are completely dry, you have a few choices on how to approach your collage. You may use white gesso with a dry brush and sweep a coat of gesso across the collage obscuring or revealing the papers below as desired. If you wish, you can then use a variety of art media to work the page surface further. If you use a stiff brush and a light hand, an effect of lines like cross-hatching can be created using white or colored gesso. You can tint your gesso with acrylic paint, or use a colored gesso to add color to your pages without concern for stickiness. Applying a clear gesso across the collaged surface can allow the papers to be seen, yet provides a surface for using other art media, including watercolors, water-soluble crayons, or pencils.

ADHESIVES

Among the most commonly used adhesives for paper are glue sticks, acrylic gel medium, and PVA glue. Be sure, when adhering with glues, to burnish the pages.

For heavier items or metal pieces, most of our contributing artists use E6000, a strong craft and hobby glue. Spend a couple of moments reading the labels of various glues at the craft to find the right adhesives to use for a variety of purposes. Use the correct adhesive for the job.

Thin papers, such as tissue or rice paper, can be rendered nearly transparent by adhering them to a surface with a liquid acrylic medium. Apply the liquid acrylic medium to both sides of the paper. Note: Do not burnish these pages! The fragile papers become even more fragile when dampened.

TIP

For good adherence and to keep bubbles from forming under the papers, burnish the glued papers firmly into place with a brayer, razor blade, or old plastic gift or credit card. To prevent scratching the surface, lay a piece of waxed paper, deli tissue, or acetate over the collaged page before burnishing.

Tina Abbott uses paper strips to add line and draw the eye quickly over the page, implying movement.

IMAGE TRANSFERS

Image transferring is the process of creating an image on an art surface by transferring it from another surface. Image transfers allow you to change the way the image appears and are great to add to art journal pages. The beauty of a transfer is in its imperfections—if you want an exact copy of an image, it's better to use the image itself, rather than a transfer. A transfer changes the image in unpredictable ways and is often missing the details. Once you have a transferred an image, you can continue to work with it, by painting over it or working into it with markers and pencil, or you can leave the transfer just the way it appears.

There are a number of methods for image transfers and various products on the market. The two techniques described here use readily available and relatively nontoxic materials: prints from your ink-jet printer and acrylic gel medium.

The right side of this journal page spread was created by doing a full-page image transfer. A second image transfer was then cut out and adhered to the page. Pencil work was added to integrate the page and text added.

In this journal, from a teaching trip to Asilomar State Park in California, both image and image transfer are used to tell a story.

HE OFFERS YOU WINGS   AND ASKS THE QUESTION—
CAN YOU FORGET YOUR FEAR OF FALLING LONG ENOUGH TO?

Image Transfers
Using Regular Gel Medium

Materials

- ink-jet print on regular copier paper (do not use photo paper; the technique will not work)
- regular gel acrylic medium, glossy
- journal page
- brayer or old credit card
- clean, damp rag
- small dish of clean water

1. Cut the ink-jet-printed image from the paper.
2. Coat the *printed surface* with the regular gel medium.

3. Place the image, coated side down, onto your journal page. Burnish firmly with a brayer or credit card. Avoid getting gel medium on the back side of the paper.
4. Clean up around the image with a damp rag, right away.
5. Allow the image to dry completely. A dry image will not feel cool to your cheek.
6. Dip your fingers into the dish of water, dampen a small area of the back of the image, and begin to rub away the paper. The wet paper will form little pills or rolls as it rubs off. Continue to work this way, dampening and then rubbing off the paper, until the whole transfer is exposed. White, cloudy areas that remain as the transfer dries indicate spots in which the paper has not been completely removed. Dampen the area and rub some more.
7. Clean up the image with a clean, damp rag.

Image Transfers
Using Soft Gel Medium

Materials

- ink-jet print on regular copier paper (do not use photo paper; the technique will not work)
- soft gel acrylic medium, matte
- journal page
- brayer or old credit card
- clean, damp rag

1. Cut the ink-jet-printed image from the paper.
2. Coat the *printed surface* with the soft gel medium.
3. Place the image, coated side down, onto your journal page. Burnish firmly with a brayer or credit card. Avoid getting gel medium on the back side of the paper.
4. Rub the back of the image with a damp rag, right away.
5. Lift the printed paper off, leaving behind your image transfer.
6. Allow to dry.

The left side of this journal spread by the author features an image transfer of a tree, and a horizon line was built using acrylics. The figure was cut from another photograph, added to the page, and handcolored.

KEEPER OF THE FLAME

An Interview with Gina Armfield

Gina Armfield is a painter, photographer, art journaler, and workshop instructor from Malibu, California.

How did you come to art journaling?

I have kept an art journal of sorts in the past, but it was called a sketchbook or a morgue (a term used in art school for a book of collected images as references for future projects). Then, I took a workshop specifically on visual journaling.

What content do you bring to your journal pages? Are they personal?

My journals are a way for me to pour out my thoughts and emotions in a subconscious way. They are a sort of art therapy—a way of exploring my inner self. I often use a photographic image over and over again in my work to show continuity.

Do you ever use your journals to process your life? How do you address comfort and privacy?

I definitely use my journals as a way to process my life. I am not a big "writer"—it's a scary thing for me to put my thoughts and feelings into written words, but I do feel very safe doing it with my art. I suppose if you knew me well, you could interpret the pages, but they are not explicit in their meaning.

You use your photography beautifully in your work. Why is that so important to what you do?

I am a painter and a photographer; that has always been my focus. I have combined those two elements for the past twenty years in my work; they are not mutually exclusive. I usually work with black and white images or an altered photo image. It's important for the image to become one with my background and to meld into a piece as a whole. I use pencils, paint, and pastel to draw into and out from the image onto the page. I use this same technique in my paintings as well.

What advice do you give your students about developing their authentic creative voice?

Developing your own voice is hard—taking what you have learned and reinterpreting it so that it's authentic to you, putting part of your soul into your work. I don't want my work to look like someone else's. I want a person to look at a piece and see *me* in the art. This doesn't mean artists can't be influenced by other artists. When I take a class from someone, I go in with the idea that I will be exposed to a new way of seeing and to learn an array of fresh techniques. I then take what I have learned and apply my own style to it. This might include using a different color palette or a variety of my own images.

I use my own photographic images in my work. This alone makes a piece uniquely mine. There's something about the black and white image that adds an edge to your work. I print mine on matte photo paper and, sometimes, even plain white copier paper. This allows me to draw, color, and write over the image. Another way to put your stamp on your work is to use the self-portrait. I believe this allows us to look inside ourselves—how we see ourselves. Not only is this a great way to introspect, but also it allows us to express our voices silently through an image.

Gina Armfield works with her own photographs to create unique journal pages. She adds her images, which are often manipulated in Photoshop, to her pages and further works on them with paint, pastels, and artist crayons to create rich, color-laden journals.

DRAWING ONTO IMAGES

When creating content on your pages with imagery, whether you are working with found images or with your own photographs, drawing onto and around them gives them greater impact and helps integrate them into the page.

You can use charcoal, colored pencils, pastels, oil pastels, markers—just about any mark-making material you have on hand—to draw onto an image. You can also use acrylic paint—just remember to treat the surface so your pages don't stick together. A matte finish spray or light coat of wax, such as Dorland's wax medium, can help. If you live in an area with very high levels of humidity, however, you might continue to have problems with pages that have been worked on with acrylic paints sticking to each other.

Use regular copier paper for printing or copying your images—the paper is readily available, and you can make multiple copies for little expense. You can alter the images in photo-editing software before printing or simply lighten them using a copier. Print three or four extra copies of your image and try a variety of techniques. As you practice, you will gain confidence. You might find that all of your practice images turn out to be excellent journal fodder.

The easiest way to begin, if you are new to the technique of drawing onto images, is to look over your image and choose areas you want to highlight, then outline these major features with pencils, pastels, or markers. You can work with colors that blend in, colors that contrast, or with black and white tones.

If you don't want to work *onto* an image, it's often useful to draw marks *around* an image. Drawing onto and around the edges of the image onto the page removes the image's white edges and helps integrate the image into the composition. China markers, Stabilo pencils, colored pencils, and crayons are useful for integrating an image. If you want an image to stand off the page, try drawing around it with a medium in a contrasting color. Gel pens and markers work well for offering a contrasting line.

This journal cover makes use of an image on which colored pencil work has been used.

The self-portrait in the lower right corner
of this spread was printed out very light
in tone and then worked in pencil and
china marker.

This image was printed large, covered
with tissue, using acrylic medium, and
then drawn into with china marker.

PRINTING ONTO TISSUE PAPER

Another method for integrating images into a page is to print them onto tissue paper. The thinness of the paper allows the edges of the image to more easily blend into the page. You can print onto tissue paper using your home ink-jet printer.

Materials

- repositionable spray adhesive
- plain copier paper
- clean piece of cardboard
- tissue paper (colors, except very dark colors, are fine)
- images to print

1. Lightly spray a piece of plain copier paper with repositionable spray adhesive. Press the sticky side to a clean piece of cardboard, then remove the paper; repeat.

2. Now place the sticky side of the copier paper against a sheet of tissue. Smooth down the tissue, then trim the page to 8.5" x 11" (21.5 x 28 cm). You are now ready to print.

3. Remove all the other paper from your printer's feed tray. Insert your tissue-copier paper sheet and print your image. You can remove the tissue paper image from its copier paper backing and use it in a collage or leave it as is to store it for later use.

These two journal pages feature self-portraits created using images printed onto tissue paper and incorporated into collages. The image on the left is the author, and on the right is artist Judi Delgado.

Just know

PHOTOGRAPHS

Photography is the easiest way to produce original imagery for use in your art journals. You don't need an expensive SLR digital camera to produce wonderful photographs; a digital point-and-shoot works just fine.

Your unique voice comes through in your images. Photograph everything: the eggs you boiled for lunch, the snail making its way down a mayapple leaf, your child's smile, the moon, a summer evening, a winter's snowfall, your waiting mailbox . . . you have amazing stuff right in your path.

Many of us have computer files filled with images we love but only see on our computer screen. It's well worth your time to print these images and add them to an art journal. They are a record of how you see your life and your part of the world. You'll often find that your images, when looked at in hindsight, tell much more about you and what you were thinking than you realized.

Once you have a pool of images, you can edit them using photo-editing software. Although most computers come with installed software, websites that allow you to edit your images for free are also an option. Even if you are limited to such edit functions as enlarging, reducing, converting to black and white, and adjusting brightness, you have a formidable array of tools.

Of course, you can't print without paper. A trip to an office supply store will reveal a variety of photo paper choices: glossy, high-gloss, satin, and matte finishes. Each paper gives a different result, so you'll want to experiment with them. One brand of glossy paper might scratch easily, despite package claims to the contrary; use that scratchable surface to your advantage by scratching around and over your photo in an "artistic" way and then spraying the image with a clear acrylic spray. Matte paper offers an interesting finish on which to work, and it receives paint and gesso well. Often, you can find double-sided matte paper, which means you can print on the other side of your outtakes, saving paper and money. You can also run art paper through your printer. I often print onto Rives BFK printmaking paper.

Tips for Better Photos

- Read your camera manual. Really. It is *full* of useful information, such as how to adjust your settings, what to do with a backlit subject, and how to delete images.

- Keep the camera set at the highest level of quality/resolution and obtain a larger memory card.

- Don't use your flash. Buy a tripod and use it when the light is low. You *can* photograph the moon, you know.

- Fill your frame with your subject. Photographing your friend as she sits in your living room? Step forward until your friend fills the frame. Step back a couple of steps, look again. Do you want a head shot? A full-size shot of her seated? A photo of her hands folded on her lap? Do you really need to include the background chair, the floor, the wall, the lamp, the window? Probably not.

- Take many photographs—twenty of one subject is not too many. Vary your approaches, such as the angle or your distance from the subject.

- Use the "delete" function on your camera and the delete key on your computer.

These two journal spreads predominantly feature photographs on painted paper pages. Printing images as large as the page offers a big impact.

PHOTO ART JOURNALS

If you take photographs regularly, keeping an art journal filled with photographs might appeal to you. Perhaps you have a plethora of images stored on your computer or on disk. Photo art journals can bring those images out of storage and onto juicy journal pages. Using your own photographs on your art journal pages gives your work your own distinctive voice.

Photo art journals are much like coffee-table books filed with your own photographs. You can add writings, quotes, and memorabilia, and you can paint or collage the backgrounds or leave them plain, but the dominant feature of this type of journal is the photography. Fill books chronologically or around a topic, such as self-portraits, or a season, such as winter. Adding images to a "regular" art journal is wonderful, of course, but keeping a specific photo art journal can provide some interesting insights into your life and surroundings.

Mary Ann Moss's journals are usually full of her photos and these travel journal pages are no exception. She used decorative stitching on the pages, sewed them to scraps of fabric and paper, and added them to a binder in varying sizes.

PRINTMAKING

Printmaking techniques can be applied to journal pages to create an interesting starting surface and background, as well as to add images to pages. Many artists use hand-carved stamps or printing blocks to add their own personal touch to their work. Easy-to-carve, soft, rubber blocks and Speedball carving tools and blade sets are available at art supply and craft stores. To stamp the images, you can use printing inks, acrylic paints, craft paints, and ink pads. Stamp pads with permanent ink, such as StazOn stamp pads, stamp over surfaces that have been painted with acrylic paints and dry completely. Interesting, decorative stamps and wooden Indian fabric printing blocks can be used to make wonderful patterns on surfaces and over images.

Many materials at home can be repurposed to print paper. Potatoes can be cut in half and the exposed surfaces carved to make stamps. Bottle caps can be stamped into paint and then stamped onto paper. The mesh bags in which onions and oranges are sold can be used to create a pattern in paint. Rolling pins can be wrapped in rubber bands or string and rolled across the paper to create larger scaled patterns. Excellent tutorials for making your own printing blocks and stamps abound on the Internet and on YouTube. *Print & Stamp Lab* by Traci Bunkers (also by Quarry Books) is a great reference on making handmade print and stamps tools from recycled items.

Monoprinting is another printing technique that can be adapted to journal pages. By using gelatin monoprinting, color, pattern, and imagery can be added to journal pages in a way that is both fun and inexpensive. Gelatin monoprinting uses a printing plate made by filling a tray or cookie sheet with unflavored gelatin made according to the juice blocks instructions, omitting the juice. You can monoprint your papers before binding them into a journal, or you can simply lay an open journal page directly onto the gelatin printing plate.

After creating pages for a travel journal using scraped paints, reductive stenciling and printmaking techniques were used to add an extra layer of color and texture.

To create this page spread in a travel journal, the pages were painted first and set aside. A gelatin plate was inked with paint. Large vinyl self-adhesive letters were placed on the plate. Another color of paint was applied to the paint. The letters were removed and then paper was laid over to make the print.

A gelatin monoprint using a scrapbook die cut as a stencil was applied to this page.

GELATIN MONOPRINTING

Materials

- unflavored gelatin
- cookie sheet
- brayer
- acrylic craft paint, liquid acrylics
- scrap paper or newspapers
- stencils, natural items such as leaves or ferns, scrapbooking die cuts, foam craft stamps
- bucket of water
- paper towels
- journal pages

1. Mix the gelatin according to the instructions for juice blocks, omitting the juice and replacing it with water.

2. Pour the mixture into a cookie sheet and allow to set up undisturbed. If you live in a warm climate, you might need to refrigerate the gelatin. Once firm, the gelatin functions as a printing plate.

3. Squeeze a small amount of paint onto the printing plate and roll a brayer over it to spread the paint evenly across the surface. If you have too much paint, lay a piece of scrap paper onto the plate and lift it off.

4. Place a stencil over the inked surface, then add a light coat of a second color over the stencil and the exposed areas.

5. Remove the plastic stencil and put it into your bucket of water.

6. Place your journal page or spread face down onto the gelatin plate. Lift off. You have a print. Usually, you will have enough paint on the plate to make at least one more print.

7. Using wet paper towels, gently wipe the gelatin plate clean for additional use.

TIP

You can imprint the paint with a foam craft stamp, draw into it with a brush, or use leaves or ferns to create nature prints. Large peel-and-stick letters also work well and allow you to add words to your prints.

KEEPER OF THE FLAME
AN INTERVIEW WITH ARTIST AND WORKSHOP INSTRUCTOR LIESEL LUND

Artist Liesel Lund is a painter, jewelry artist, textile artist, workshop instructor and an avid art journaler.

You come to art with a rich personal history, steeped in art from childhood. Can you tell us about your background and how it impacts your artwork today?

I had a wonderful childhood for an artist. I had creative role models around me. My nana made beautiful ceramic beads which she sold in her shop and at a national arts and crafts fair. She was also a gifted weaver and embroidery and appliqué artist. My mom is an amazing traditional quilter, teacher, and author. I grew up with piles of richly colored fabrics and patchwork spread out on the living room floor. They taught me to "see" the world through artists' eyes. When I expressed an interest in drawing, I was given art supplies and lots of encouragement. As an only child I had a lot of time to create, imagine things and read, all of which also nourished my creativity. Later, when I went to a liberal arts college, I studied art and later took classes at local art schools. As a result, I feel that I'm both self taught and also have had formal training. Although it's useful to know how other artists work, I enjoy diving into things and figuring them out for myself.

I think that I got this "can do" attitude from being around my family and observing the women striking out in their own creative endeavors. I don't expect everyone to like the work I do. I just make it to please myself. Both my mom and nana worked that way, too. One thing I learned early in my jewelry-making days was that, regardless of how the necklace was constructed, everyone preferred the one made with their favorite colors. This was so helpful, because I now know not take it personally when someone doesn't like my work; it just means that the piece doesn't match their personal aesthetic.

Using vibrant, rich color reminiscent of textile designs, Liesel Lund creates lush images on her journal pages.

Your journal pages are very vibrant and expressive. You seem to paint your experience and your feelings. Can you tell us a bit about your journaling process?

Journaling is a wonderfully freeing process for me. I love making it loose and messy and outside any "rules." I make an effort to not care about what it looks like and just let it evolve. Working with my hands is a great way to balance out all that computer graphics time I spent on the job, creating designs to please others. Journals are just for me. Often, words can't fully express my thoughts or feelings, so I let the colors and images "talk." It's a place to explore new ideas and to play with my materials in new ways.

I often don't know what I'm going to do when I start. I have found that, for me, it's best just to jump in: grab a favorite color of paint, pencil, or marker and make some marks, change colors, change mediums, toss in scraps of paper, draw over those—let the lines and shapes just flow. I think of my art making as a conversation. Each step responds to the last one, while introducing a new thought or idea. I like this because it evolves in delightful ways that I couldn't have planned from the beginning, and it feels like a more authentic expression of whatever I'm thinking and feeling. Sometimes, I'll just want to repeat a shape, like leaves or spirals or dots, over and over. There is something so satisfying in just letting yourself do whatever you want, regardless of whether it makes sense to anyone else. Some of my journals have themes, like what it is like to be in the ocean, and others are open to anything. Sometimes I don't even create the pages sequentially. I just skip around.

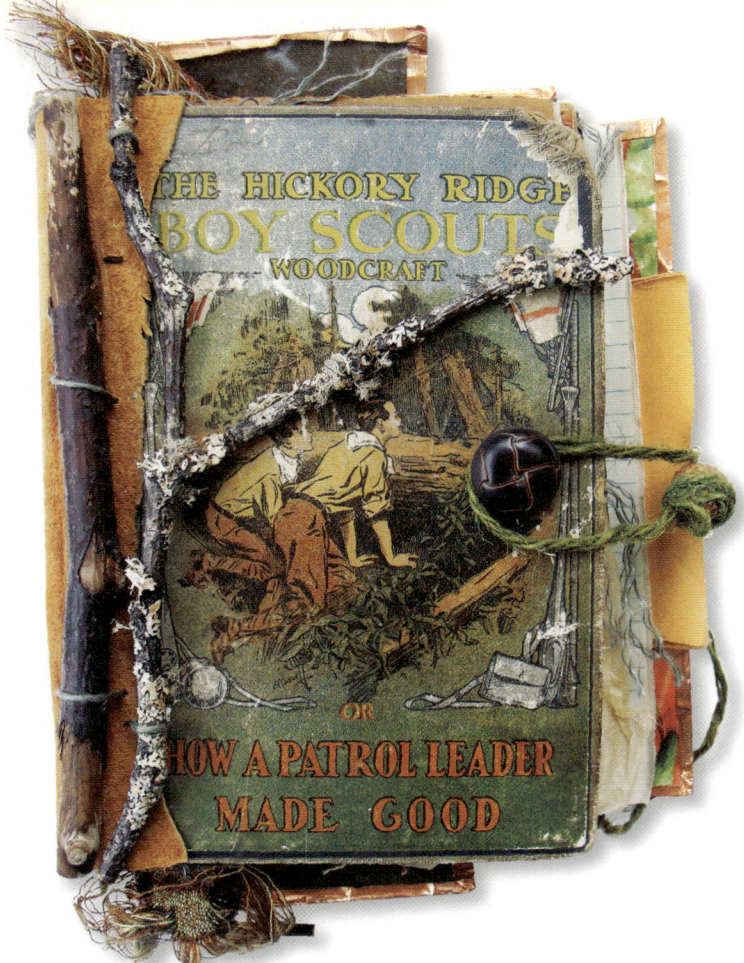

Laden with nature imagery and photographs, this art journal uses multiple approaches to create a unified whole—paper choice, color palette, book cover, and three-dimensional embellishments.

My process feels very intuitive. Often I will see a theme emerging over several pages with a depth and emotion that I was unaware of. I create best when I'm alone, listening to good music, drinking tea, and just playing loosely with my materials. Sometimes I start with an emotion, theme, or dream that I want to explore. Other times I start with the paint and see what happens. I've taken photos of journal pages as they've progressed and I highly recommend everyone doing this. It is amazing to see all the different stages. When I've shown the photos to people they've told me that as they looked at each stage they think, "Stop! That looks great. Don't keep going–you'll ruin it . . . " and then they see the next stage and they like that too, and finally at the end, they like that photo the best. But you have to be willing to keep taking risks and push your art until it "feels" done.

You work in a number of mediums: paintings, jewelry, and textiles, in addition to work on the pages of books. How do these influence your art journals and vice versa?

I don't use my works in any intentional way to influence each other but they do unconsciously inform one another. I was amused recently when I realized that I had used the same flower shape in my journal page, on a handbag, and in a tin charm necklace. Aesthetically, all my mediums share commonalities. They all have lots of different colors, textures, and layers. All my art is very full and rich. I like a lot going on visually so that one's eye is kept busy taking in all the details. I've discovered that regardless of which medium I'm working in, my favorite part of the creative process is from the middle to the end. This is because by the middle, I've established the colors and theme and have more than one layer down, and its gets more visually exciting to me as I go along, adding more richness and texture to it. I used to worry that by not "specializing" in one medium that I wouldn't develop my skill as quickly. But what I've come to realize is that each medium keeps my creating fresh and that my visual language keeps evolving. No matter how long I live I won't have time to try out all the ideas I have!

Images of ocean life fill Liesel's journals on the sea. Pages feature window-like openings in which to peer and look for more.

CHAPTER 4:
BURSTING INTO FLAMES: CREATING MEANINGFUL CONTENT

Art journals are by their very nature intended for meaningful content; the word "journal" implies a record of some sort—of reactions to events and experiences, of feelings about people or situations, of a connection to an idea or a story, or even of places we've been in our dreams and imaginings. All that we have stored inside our hearts and minds can be brought to bear on our art journal pages. Our lives are rich and full and worthy of exploration. Even the mundane details of daily living can tell an important story about us. When we spill our experiences onto our pages using art, we give power to our artistic voice. We reach into our day-to-day existence and examine it in ways that are unique; with color and line, shape, and texture.

One of my previous books, *True Vision: Authentic Art Journaling*, though it shared some techniques, largely focused on filling the artwork we use in our journal pages with personal, meaningful content. Doing so in a way that's unique to us, true to our voice, and created with our own visual language is what makes this an artistic process. Consider the techniques described in this book—choosing a journal, applying paint or ink to the pages, adding images you've made or found, and working those images with markers or pens or crayon—these activities, these processes, constitute the words of your visual vocabulary. You speak volumes, before you even so much as consider the addition of text, through the visual elements on your pages. Color, line, and shape: these elements all tell stories.

John Hammons created a journal specifically to explore portraiture.

The portrait is another one of John Hammons' explorations of painting the face.

SOURCES FOR JOURNAL FODDER

Journal fodder is literally everywhere. Some art journalers gather scraps and snippets throughout their daily travels, even off the sidewalk. Collecting evidence of your daily existence is one way to gather journaling material. Candy Jernigan, an artist who was part of New York's avant-garde movement, created journals of things she found on New York City streets and on trips abroad. She included the usual things, such as ticket stubs, but she also included pop tabs, somewhat-horrifying crack vials from her neighborhood, and dead bugs found when she opened up her summer home.

Journal fodder also arrives in the daily mail: magazines, catalogs, advertisements, and newspapers can provide visual elements for journal page collages and silhouettes for use as images or stencils. Artist Carla Sonheim uses junk mail materials as paper pages in her journals and often creates layered art journal using junk mail papers of varying sizes.

Digital cameras offer what was once the exclusive purview of the Polaroid camera—instant images. Shoot, download, and print them in a flash—depending on the model, you can even print directly from your camera. Printers are getting smaller and smaller, made to be portable for travel purposes. Computers often come equipped with photo-editing software, and upgraded software is available at reasonable prices. The world is your oyster, the printed image your pearl.

All-in-one printers that copy, scan, and print offer limitless permutations of any one image. A single image can be scanned, altered—in color, size, or contrast or by using special effects—with photo-editing software, and printed out as many times as you like. Working with repetition, using one image multiple times, for a forceful effect is very accessible. A scrap of a grocery list left behind in a grocery cart can be copied, enlarged, reversed, and manipulated into the perfect item for a journal page. The possibilities for journal fodder are endless.

Using found papers, ephemera from her daily life, and personalized photographs, Elizabeth Bunsen creates layered yet cohesive journal pages.

EVERYDAY AND TOPICAL JOURNALS

An everyday art journal is for ordinary, everyday subject matter. Although not necessarily one you work in every day, it is a journal that encompasses life. Perhaps it's a record of many things, without a narrowed focus. A topical journal is an art journal *with* a specific focus. Travel, nature, childhood or parenthood, a life change, a season, a person, or an exploration of a favorite artist are examples of topics for a topical art journal.

Many art journalers work in both kinds of journals simultaneously, because one type of journal isn't necessarily better than the other. An everyday journal provides the opportunity to create a journaling practice; you can include in it anything that strikes your artistic fancy. In a topical journal, you can explore a significant event or subject in as much depth as you want. The advantage of any art journal—topical or everyday—is that it closes; your work is not on public display, leaving you free to experiment, explore, and plumb the depths of an idea.

By using drawing, painting, mark-making, stenciling, and stamping with her hand-carved stamps, Elizabeth integrates all the paper surfaces on the pages into a whole.

KEEPER OF THE FLAME:

AN INTERVIEW WITH ELIZABETH BUNSEN

Elizabeth Bunsen's art journal practice is an integral part of her spiritual practice. Her journals shine with her divine spark, expressed in eloquent images and small phrases. I asked Elizabeth if she might talk about art journaling and the divine spark:

I have been writing, doodling, and sticking stuff in journals for more than thirty-five years, now. My passions, pleasures, and disappointments coexist in these spiral notebooks with drawings of table settings, street scenes, portraits of friends, and ideas for art projects. A very precious journal has taped to the pages violets and other wildflowers from the spring that I was pregnant with my only child. Another little black journal with a Greek goddess on the cover documents my fears and trepidation about learning to work in a newly rented studio while my son embraced preschool.

My journals receive, document, and preserve my path through this life. During the past several years, that documentation has become increasingly visual and layered. My journals carry my night and day dreams, and as my trusted friends, they remind me to "feel good now," to "find joy," to let my passion be radiant, to be here now, and to hold this moment with love and reverence.

About nine or ten years ago, I began practicing yoga in earnest and my life shifted in new and unexpected ways. My practice has waxed and waned over the years, but I make a point to journal after yoga, and I find the sweetest jewels as a result. Increasingly, journaling for me is a kind of creative meditation or yoga. I often create little rituals around sitting down with pen and page: I light a candle and some incense, brew some tea, and put on some of what my thirteen-year-old son calls "woo woo" music, then I write, paint, print, stamp, paste, and maybe glue down a few sequins. My journal and I do the Wah dance of "love holding love holding love . . . ." This movement from outer nature to inner reveling is how I "be, dream, and play" in this ecstatic world. I feel that my path is to find, document, augment, and share this beauty. This is the divine spark I court, and this spark often sets my heart on fire. I try to savor, sustain, and express these moments on the page.

Elizabeth Bunsen's daily journal practice is infused with her daily life, including her spiritual practice.

This page in an everyday journal from Elizabeth Bunsen shows a simple grid layout covered with successive layers of writing, paint, more writing, imagery and embellishment.

This art journal, by Mary Ann Moss, is a topical journal related to her travels in Italy and is created using a variety of papers, pockets, photos, and binder rings for ultimate portability.

RESEARCHING A TOPIC AS A CREATIVE FIRE-STARTER

Gathering information and imagery for a subject can certainly fan the flames of inspiration. When choosing a subject, consider ways of doing research. If you are traveling, go beyond the travel guides and maps—scour eBay, for example, or used-bookstores and flea markets for vintage travel ephemera, such as metal charms, postcards, children's books on the state or country, vintage travel guides or language guides, and vintage history books. Choose colors for your page surfaces; if you're unfamiliar with the landscape you're traveling to, check out images on the Web to develop a color palette.

If your topical journal is something less concrete and more personal, such as a life change, your research might include information from books you've found helpful, photos and images of past events, or quotes and prose on the subject. If you want to work in a more symbolic way, shoot photos that represent your feelings: a flowing river, for example, can communicate that change is a constant.

Often, when working on a topical journal, I keep a basket handy, tossing into it all manner of related items. Images from books and magazines, quick prints of photos I've taken that I want to remember to use, snips of decorative paper and fabric in color palettes that work, found objects that seem to connect with my topic, ephemera that I have tracked down on eBay or in antique shops . . . all make their way into the basket. When I sit down to work, I sift through the contents and choose things that need to be used right then, when the creative energy is high. Some good advice: don't treat the materials you have gathered as too precious to use!

L. K. Ludwig used a vintage children's book on Florida as a source of imagery then repurposed the covers to house the journal.

BEGIN WITH THE MASTERS

The advice most often given to new art journalers is to make journal pages—in other words, to work in your journal often, and practice, practice, practice. The more frequently you work, the more your own style evolves and the more artistic skills you add to your visual vocabulary. If you're stumped on where to begin, begin with the masters. Who are the masters? The masters are artists you admire. Perhaps they're artists commonly acknowledged as masters: Gustav Klimt, Vincent Van Gogh, Georgia O'Keeffe, or Edward Weston. But they might also be artists whose work you have come to admire through a trade publication or the Internet. It matters not. What matters is making a commitment to learn as much as you can by practicing in the pages of your journal.

Your art journal is a great place to practice visual vocabulary and build your artistic language. Study the master's art you admire: what draws you to it? Is it the color palette? Are you intrigued with the way the artist builds layers? Is it his or her astonishing use of light? Dissect, analyze—not just the artwork but also your response to the artwork. Read about the artist and his or her life, if you can. How does that master's experience come through in the work? Although your life experience is your own, and you cannot assume the mantle of the artist's life, you can practice in your art journal the visual vocabulary he or she uses.

Perhaps you want to try out Georgia O'Keeffe's bold use of color. Ask yourself how the color choices make you feel. What subject matter can you draw from your own life to practice with those colors? Perhaps it's the way an admired artist builds dark, mysterious layers. Practice building layers about your own dark mysteries with tissue, paint, paper, and marks.

Perhaps the artist works with figures, whose emotion draws you in. What draws you to the figures? How can you represent a figure in a way that comes from within you? You can make figures by drawing, painting, collage, or photography. Are you drawn in by the way the artist fills the page, the scale of the work, the personal writings? Copying to learn is a time-honored artistic practice, but at some point you need to move beyond imitation and ask yourself these kinds of questions. If you continue to copy, you simply are not making personal, meaningful content.

This painting by John Hammons pays homage to Vermeer's Girl with a Pearl Earring.

Misty Mawn's distinctive style often crops up in her students' later work as they begin to internalize what they have learned in her painting classes.

In this unusually sized (long and narrow) journal by Misty Mawn, she explores new ideas for working with figures, landscapes, and still life.

FANNING THE FLAMES: FACING DOWN CREATIVE BLOCK

When facing creative block, you'll hear, "It happens to everyone!" This response is annoying but true. Sooner or later, all artists hit a bump or a block. Here are some suggestions for managing creative block:

- Accept that you'll experience this at some point, and be proactive. On those days when you're overflowing with more ideas than you can possibly work on, make a list of them; add details so you can recall the train of thought related to that idea.

- Allow the block to be. Sometimes, the more we push against it, the emptier our mind seems to be. Do something else for a while: take long walks or work on a more mindless project, such as organizing your closets, knitting a scarf, or rearranging the studio.

- Work. Sometimes you just have to work your way through a block. My husband, also an artist, calls it "getting the ugly out of the way." You might make work that you hate—it's okay. Toss it. Don't let that work stand in your way. Keep going. Even if you throw out the next seven things, you might discover that the eighth thing is IT. I've found that this process is almost a dialogue between myself and my inner critic's wacky expectations. If I just keep working and accept what comes out (and I don't have to keep it), then it becomes okay to work, and the real work emerges.

- As clichéd as it sounds, *look* around. Go to the library, the book store, a museum show, a jam-packed gallery. Page through books and magazines, look at paintings—not to figure out what to do, or even to gather ideas, but simply to feed your creative self.

- Books on writing, particularly those with writing prompts, make excellent creativity starters for personal, meaningful journal pages. Have a couple of these on hand. You can find them in the reference section of the bookstore.

amidst the tempest tossed to and fro. Herald Fall begins to pass us by. Yet, far off though is the coming of Spring.

Frosty mornings greet the days. And all of a sudden Winter came.

Tracie Lyn Huskamp's journal page feature drawn, painted, and penned nature scenes.

for it is only in fables and fairytales that such a place exists...

this meadow where dreams flutter about only to light upon the soft delicate petals of our imaginations and drowsy days invite us to linger.

—ode to a meadow

the seasons blanket these months, days, each moment with the smiles, laughter, and tears of life.

Oh heavenly garden sparkling in the sunlight. Bejeweled and dazzling like a precious gem, all glittered and shiny with colors of the rainbow to entertain.

Each flora and fauna dancing in the breezes of these hot summer days swaying to the rhythms of the wind.

You beguiled us with your chorus.

—june ballet in the garden

I walked beside the hedgerow and tangled along the fence, which leads to the farmer's field, grew wild brambles and prickleberries.

As I passed, they came forth to greet me, coaxed out of the shadows into the sunlight by the neighboring pansies, who invited me to stay for tea, this fine morning. Knowing how partial I am to sweets and the company of flowers.

These pages from Tracie Lyn Huskamp's journal feature delicate nature drawings and lyrical text.

BUILDING A PAGE THAT WORKS FOR YOU

If you're still asking, "What do I do?" try this: go back through the previous chapters and try out a technique, tip, or idea from each. Choose a journal, select some art supplies, create a surface on the page, add some imagery related to some personal content. Just keep adding paint or images or marks or writing, until your eye tells you that it's enough.

You might find your pages cluttered, too busy for your own taste, even when you're going for a very layered look. If so, it's time to consider composition. Composition is the "putting together," the arrangement, of the visual elements on your page; it's your "page layout." When composing your page layout, you need to consider visual elements such as line, shape, texture, color, size, perspective, space—positive and negative—and direction (the way the art directs your eye across the page: vertical, horizontal, or diagonal).

Many artists use their instinct to make decisions about how they use line and shape, color and size, deciding, as they work, which visual elements take priority over others. Part of the artistic process is deciding which elements are to become visually dominant. The artist decides on the focus, the center of interest, of the piece and arranges elements around the focus. Applying paint and image in layers to draw attention to a particular place: this is part and parcel of the art-journal process.

Following are some techniques that can help you achieve composition in your art journal pages and spreads: the rule of thirds, the rule of odds, and the concept of simplification.

The **rule of thirds:** rather than bisecting your piece—dividing it into two equal sections—imagine dividing your page or spread into three equal sections and place your focal piece near one of the lines. When you place an object at the center of the image, you bisect it. All attention is drawn to the center, and the viewer's eye doesn't look beyond the center. Placing an object near one of the trisecting lines gives the

piece more tension, energy, and interest than simply centering the object would.

The **rule of odds:** surrounding your focal piece with an even number of objects creates a visually comforting arrangement. Conversely, breaking this rule and using a single image alone creates tension in a piece.

Simplification: paring down a page to its essential elements to communicate a message—shooting a photograph in which the central image is in focus and the background is out of focus, for example, or creating a painting with a highly detailed focal image and a background of looser, larger brush strokes.

Artists often intentionally break these "rules" to help their work communicate and idea or feeling. For example, the goal might be to create something unpleasant or disturbing, to provide a sort of visual cognitive dissonance. You can find many useful reference materials on composition at libraries and bookstores. Information is also available online.

In this journal page spread by John Hammons, the self-portrait is deliberately not placed in the center of the spread. Placing the portrait off to one side creates more energy and interest in the composition.

KEEPER OF THE FLAME:

AN INTERVIEW WITH TEESHA AND TRACY MOORE

Teesha and Tracy Moore are recognized as pivotal forces in the art-journal movement, hosting national mixed-media retreats, including an event just for art journaling called, aptly, Journalfest. I asked them about the creative practice of art journaling.

How did you begin art journaling?

Teesha: I started taking classes in bookmaking, and loved what I produced but didn't know what to fill them with. I knew about the journals that one writes in, but I wasn't a writer. I was involved in mail art at the time, and realized that I had created this huge body of work that I would never see again. When people asked me what type of art I did, I found it hard to explain. So, I told myself that a *journal* can be anything I want it to be. There were no rules. I decided right there to make a visual journal and put the same type of art in it that I sent to my friends. It seemed kind of like a portfolio of my work but quickly became my "playground"—the place to play with different ideas and keep notes of the days, for example.

Tracy: Teesha had started making fascinating journals from old books and gave me one to use. It was such a work of art that I couldn't force myself to use it. I hated my handwriting, and I didn't draw at all. Anything I put in the journal was bound to ruin it. It sat on my desk for a solid year before Teesha finally gave me the ultimatum that if I didn't start using it, she would take it back. In that first journal, I still couldn't do anything on the beginning pages, so I started using rubber stamps to stamp images I liked at the back of it.

This freed me up a bit, and I started actually writing . . . in the middle of the journal, not at the beginning yet. Eventually, I started drawing in my journal. I kept everything very private for a year, then Teesha saw it sitting on my desk one day and started looking through it. When I got home that day, she told me she really liked my drawings. After that, I began making journals of my own and melded my drawings with my writing on the same page.

These two journal pages, (left), by artist Tracy Moore make extensive use of drawing, doodling, and writing for bold, graphical effect.

This journal page, (above), by Teesha Moore embodies her distinctive artistic signature with her central image, surrounded by handwritten text and a collaged border.

How did you come to acquire the practice of journaling with such frequency?

Teesha: Journaling has become an activity that I *have* to do: eating, sleeping, working, and journaling. It grounds me and reminds me of things that I *love* about life.

Tracy: Early on, I tried to section off my journal into things like "writing," "drawing" . . . . I found that this rigid structure kept me from journaling. As soon as I gave up all the rules, the doors flew open and I found that I just loved to journal for hours. Instead of just writing, I could draw, paint, collage, and carve stamps to use in my journals. The journal went everywhere with me (and still does) and is an avid source of entertainment.

What advice might you give about each person about finding their own voice through their journal pages?

Teesha: Don't edit yourself; that is the only way to learn more about yourself. Create intuitively and instinctually, and you will find your style—it will come out and surprise you. Also, practice, practice, practice. Repeatedly doing something, anything, will make you better at it. So many people want to be really good at something by spending an afternoon trying it. We want instant gratification. To really find your style, create work that sings, and get the most out of journaling, you need to spend a lot of time doing it.

Tracy: Sit back and *play* in your journal. When you have no rules, you really free yourself up to find out what you truly like and what is aching to burst forth from within you. If it's boring, you will avoid doing it.

Journal pages from husband and wife, Tracy and Teesha Moore, exemplify their unique, personal, artistic styles. Tracy's work is shown on left; Teesha's work is at right.

CHAPTER 5:

FEEDING THE FIRE: ADDING DETAILS

Once you have a visual composition laid out onto your journal page and your creative fire is crackling merrily, the next step is to add detail and/or text to your journal pages, feeding your creative fire further. Adding this next layer of details to the page enhances the content you are developing on your journal page. These final layers can allow you to complete an idea, create a more unified and finished page, and draw the viewer in with a sense of intimacy.

There are a number of ways you can add just a bit more content to complete the idea you had in mind. Perhaps you need to express yourself in words and find that adding text in some form completes the journaling process and the page for you. Text can be used as both a literal and a graphic element, giving it flexibility and significance. A single word on a page can have great impact. Or, perhaps you have serendipitously come across something more three-dimensional, such as a smooth twig, some fabulous fabric trim, or a mysterious bit of tumbled beach glass that seems apropos to the content so you wish to work it into your page. Adding an envelope filled with related materials, or creating interesting pockets or tabs can create interactive pages where, in order to view the content completely, the viewer must open, unfold, or peer into your page. Layering your art journal with further detail can bring a piece to a place where it communicates more richly with the viewer and makes the art journaling process more satisfying.

Karen Cole's distinctive work uses copper foil tooled with her original drawings sewn to pages. The copper foil is then painted and embellished with vintage jewelry findings, metal stampings, trims, fabrics, and papers.

KEEPER OF THE FLAME:

AN INTERVIEW WITH KAREN COLE

Artist Karen Cole works with metal, paint, and embellishment in a unique and amazing way to create her art journals. I asked Karen to tell us a bit about her journey and her artistic process.

Tell me how you became connected to the alternative arts/paper arts community.

Over the years, I have morphed from a painter into a ceramicist and then into a glass artist, and now I'm dabbling in mixed media. I've kind of thrown everything into the pot and am working on a big "art stew." I find it difficult to work in one medium day in and day out.

In 2005, while I was doing fused glass "paintings," I decided to try my hand at mosaics with the leftover glass. I Googled "mosaic artists," to see what others were creating and, not long after that, I was on my way to Italy to attend a weeklong workshop with Michael De Meng. Since then, I've taken many other workshops with other wonderfully talented mixed-media artists and started collecting assorted found objects, particularly old jewelry findings and parts and smaller metal objects.

When I was a teacher in Philadelphia, I found a roll of copper sheeting in my supply closet. I read a book on copper tooling and realized I could draw into the copper. I discovered, after using found metal objects as embellishment on the copper sheet, that I needed to go back and draw some more into the metal and remembered the work I had done with my students, drawing and painting on the copper. Perfect. Stitching on the copper came later as a wonderful way to add even

more line and definition to the design. I discovered, as I began to attach objects to the copper and use the attachments as a basis for the design, that I was reminded of old illuminated manuscripts. I started actually making some of my copper sheet pieces into illuminated manuscript–style letters.

I use Golden heavy gel medium as an embellishment, because it can be applied thickly and drawn and written into, and when it dries, it can be painted over. I feel I get the look of encaustic painting (another medium I have tried) without the fumes. I can even put the gel medium on the copper.

These richly embellished pages by Karen Cole pay homage to her mother who had recently passed away. When layered, tooled, and stitched, the copper foil turns into something more jewel-like.

The portfolio is a remembrance of your mother. Art often works as a place for processing feelings and experience. Do you find that you often work from your experiences and feelings? I know your travels, whether to another country or to a flower show, seem to inspire your content.

Yes. Absolutely. I made an "Italian shoe shrine" after being inspired by a shoe in a tapestry at the Vatican. It was a detail from a very large piece—I get overwhelmed by all of the monumental artwork that exists and find that I need to narrow things down a bit. I decided to concentrate on the things that were closest to eye level: Roman sandals.

The aging of my friends, my family, and myself is paramount in my mind, these days, and I find myself working out these issues in my work. I go through old photographs, paintings, self-portraits, and jewelry parts and marvel at the changes. I comment on the years gone by with a collage, a copper drawing, or a journal page.

USING TEXT

To perceive text as a detail might seem a bit strange; in fact, text can be added at any point in the journaling process. It can be used as a background surface, a focal image, and as a detail.

The decision to add text or not to your pages often rests with issues of privacy. Many art journalers are unwilling to include written content because their journals are handled by other people, and they have concerns about the content being read. One way this concern is sometimes addressed is by rendering the writing illegible. You can do this by using unreadable handwriting: writing in a loose, loopy script that lacks definable letters allows you to express yourself in writing and make use of the

rhythmic visual element of the written word. Another approach is to write on the background in one direction then in another and another, until the writing is obscured, then begin a work over the writing. Or, write a normal journal entry, apply a coat of gesso, then begin to create over that layer, leaving some of the writing visible and obscuring as much as you want of the written part. Many artists work their text into the background so that it's still somewhat legible but can only be understood by them.

John Hammons makes use of the placement of his calligraphy to enhance the content of his page beyond merely adding text.

Handwritten words add to the intimate feeling of Leslie Marsh's pages.

IDEAS FOR TEXT APPLICATIONS

Add text detailing your worries, thoughts, hopes, dreams, prayers, imaginings, or favorite quotes to a journal page by using:

- your normal handwriting
- calligraphy
- illegible loopy script
- gel pens, brush pens, paint pens, crayons, markers
- doodle scripts
- your computer to generate and print text on various papers, tissue, or transparent materials
- collaged words, letters, or phrases cut from magazines and old books
- ink and a skewer or paint and an extra-fine brush
- spray paint and stencils
- rub-on letters and alphabet stickers
- rubber stamps of various sizes and fonts
- hand-cut printing blocks
- gelatin monoprints
- finger paints
- squeezable fabric paint or thinned acrylic paint in squeeze bottles

KEEPER OF THE FLAME:

AN INTERVIEW WITH SETH APTER

Seth Apter is an artist in New York City whose blog, the Altered Page, examines the artistic process of other artists and offers inspiring online articles related to art journals.

I've been a reader of your blog for some time and have observed that you seem to be interested in and/or intrigued by the processes of other artists: how they work, what their inspirations are, for example. Can you tell us how this curiosity influences your own artwork and your own artistic processes?

I think curiosity is the basis for most learning, discovery, and creativity. I love to explore, to analyze, to search, and to understand. This includes understanding myself and the feelings that drive the creation of my own artwork, as well as exploring others and their own underlying creativity. Making art can be a very solitary process. And I embrace this aspect of being

an artist. But I have also found creative fuel through the relationships I've made through my blog and via my artistic collaborations and online group projects. I think this sense of curiosity underlies a desire to always be growing and developing. My connections with other artists and my exploration of their own artistic process serve as powerful inspiration to me, not in terms of style or approach but more in terms of being part of a larger pool of creative energy.

The journal we're featuring here is a travel journal from a journey to Greece. It's slim and rich and has an ancient feel without an overpowering use of sepia tones or antiquing finish. There is a softness to the pages and to the paper itself. Are the choices you made in this regard conscious, or were they only visible at the close of the work? Is this a common experience when you work?

All the travel journals I make are created using the same process. They are all handmade. I create the structure for my journal before I leave for my vacation. I base the size, the cover, the paper, and the binding technique on my sense of the destination. Often a color wash is added to each page before leaving, so I don't experience the "blank page" syndrome. Usually, the pages are left unbound until I return home.

I bring a small journaling kit that I put together and always begin work on the pages while on vacation. I set aside time to work in the journal every day, because I feel the most inspiration when I am creating in the actual place that I am creating about. Part of my vacation also becomes about finding bits and pieces to add to my journal and, of course, taking pictures to include. When I return home, I complete the pages, add the journaling, and include photographs that I have printed and altered. The journal is than bound and completed.

I always try to select materials that reflect my destination. For the Greece journal, I purposely chose pages that were taken from vintage books to reflect the ancient origins of the country. I used naturally aged pages, rather than aging papers myself, to mirror the patina found in Greece that developed naturally over time. For a travel journal I made for a trip to New Mexico, as another example, I chose textured cold-press watercolor paper covered in chalky color washes to reflect the colors and textures found on the adobe buildings.

What does working in a book have to offer that might not be available from working on, say, individual canvases or sheets of paper?

Seth Apter's travel journal from his trip to Greece is filled with mementos and ephemera of that journey but created in a way that reflects his experience of the place. With the chosen color palette, the use of aged paper, and the placement and type of ephemera, Seth creates a journal that communicates on multiple levels.

My favorite art is that which tells a story or reflects an experience. There is something about the "book form" in journaling that lends itself to the concept of a story and a history—a beginning, a middle, and an end. Working in a book is like going on a journey. For me, the journey I take when creating the pages in a journal mirrors life's experiences and parallels the story I am telling. And I believe that this is true for the reader as well.

POCKETS, ENVELOPES, AND TABS

Pockets, envelopes, and tabs are structural ways to add interest and content to your journal. Pockets can be made of many materials—decorative or painted papers, cardstock, metal mesh—and can be attached to the interiors of cover boards or to individual pages. Pockets can even be created on folios and bound into a journal as part of its structure. Library pockets, the ones you used to find at the back of library books, are available from many craft stores and scrapbook suppliers. A simple pattern for a library-style pocket is shown, right, and can be enlarged for use in your journal. You can also create your own templates by taking existing pockets apart and tracing them.

Envelopes are readily obtainable and easy to use for storing items in a journal. Stationery stores and office supply stores offer an amazing variety of envelopes. Hobby shops that carry stamp-collecting supplies often carry glassine envelopes, which provide a semi-opaque view of the contents. You can increase the impact of envelopes and pockets by adorning them with art and by using them to store art. The act of opening the envelope or looking into the pocket lets the viewer interact with the content and evokes a sense of discovery.

Tabs can be purchased from office supply, craft, and scrapbooking stores. You can make your own tabs using a tab punch, also available from craft and scrapbooking stores, or by simply cutting your own. Tabs from file folders can also be repurposed for use on journal pages, and, if you apply images to the tabs, you can provide additional content beyond text.

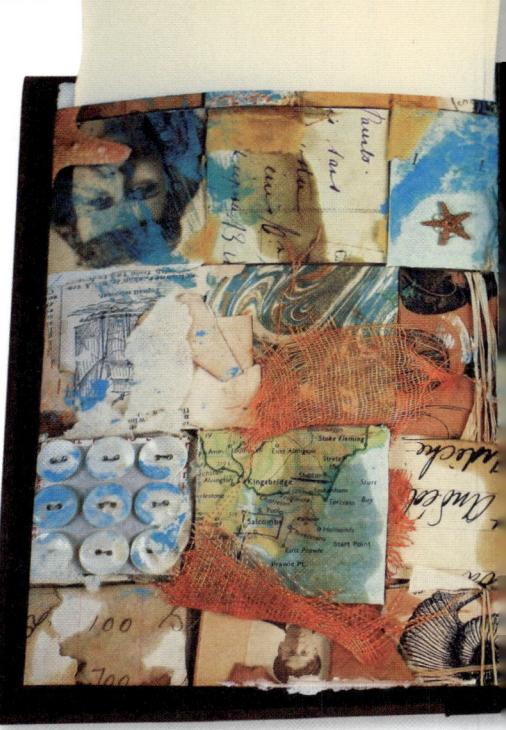

Jan Harris created this pocket in a purchased journal to hold journal fodder until she has a chance to work with it.

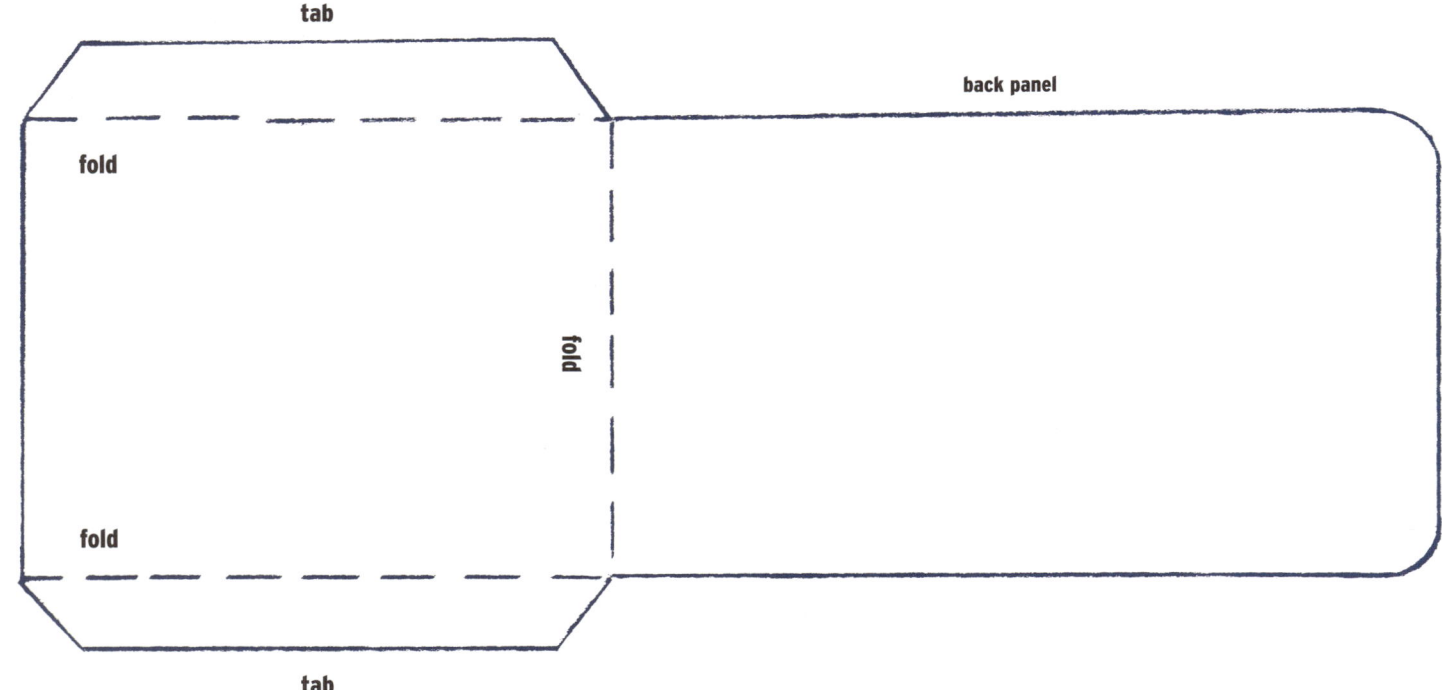

Library-style pocket template; enlarge to desired size. Fold along dotted lines, wrap the small tabs around the outside of the back panel. Glue the back panel to your journal page.

A simple paper bag can be used to create a journal page entry. Brenda Shackleford created this tipped in pocket from a bag, filled it with ephemera and journaled on the outside of it.

Judi Delgado uses paper shutters to create an interactive window.

EMBELLISHMENT

Embellishment refers to the addition of three-dimensional materials to an art journal page or cover. It's far easier to add embellishment to a book cover than to the interior pages; you can attach almost anything to a cover. When choosing what objects to attach to your interior pages, consider whether it's important to you to have your journal close flat.

Common examples of page additions are fabric, fabric trims, vintage lace, fibers, metal mesh, eyelets or grommets, small book covers, silk flowers, beads, stones, shells, beach glass, wooden shapes, metal shapes, and metal charms. The methods for attaching fabric or similar items include stitching, either by hand or by machine, and adhesive. Craft glue is an excellent adhesive for flat and porous items. Hot glue guns work well for adhering items such as flat metal shapes, seashells, and silk flowers. Craft glue designed for adhering metal and glass can also be used for other nonporous materials, such as stones and plastics. Wire wrapping is the best way to attach heavier three-dimensional objects, such as stones, and to allow charms to dangle over a page edge. Metal mesh and even metal foil can be sewn to a page surface.

When adding three-dimensional objects to a page in your art journal, try to ensure they serve a purpose or have a connection to the content. The object might serve to reinforce the color palette, for example (a decorative silk flower), offer a tactile surface (a velvet ribbon), or add content related to the subject (seashells on a travel journal page).

Leslie Marsh bound this journal by hand and carefully chose embellishments that beautifully communicate the journal's theme. An inserted window filled with feathers and vintage paper was covered with mica and wired into place. The vintage bird finding that is wired onto the cover communicates the title in a glance.

DEEP CREEK LAKE
2007

HE WHO WOULD LEARN TO FLY ONE DAY MUST FIRST LEARN TO STAND AND WALK AND CLIMB AND DANCE; ONE CANNOT FLY INTO FLYING.

– FRIEDRICH NIETZSCHE

"COME TO THE EDGE."
"WE CAN'T. WE'RE AFRAID."
"COME TO THE EDGE."
"WE CAN'T. WE WILL FALL!"
"COME TO THE EDGE."
AND THEY CAME.
AND HE PUSHED THEM.
AND THEY FLEW.

– GUILLAUME APOLLINAIRE

L. K. Ludwig adds both color and text with the tabs on these pages.

KEEPER OF THE FLAME:

AN INTERVIEW WITH JUDY WILKENFELD

Judy Wilkenfeld is a book artist from Australia. Her work is steeped in history and rich with embellished content. She researches her work heavily and uses symbols at every level of her multilayered work. I asked her to talk with us about her process.

Your work is very rich and historical. It appears to me that you do a good bit of background research, including genealogical research, on the topics you work with. Tell us why researching is so important to your work.

History and the stories of the lives and experiences of those who have come before us have always fascinated me. There is so much to learn from them. Most of my artist's books are based on facts, not fiction. The majority of my books tell those chosen stories without words, and when producing these anthologies, authenticity is critical to me. Consequently, researching and investigating are the tools with which I can achieve that legitimacy. The telling is conveyed through the use of colors, textures, and found objects, fused together in a mixed-media book form. The research facilitates the telling more fully, but it also enlightens me with new information. Because authenticity is so key for my work, I scout the world for the right pieces. The right elements are the conduits through which the story is told; the pieces become the orators who tell the story on my behalf. The fabrics, found objects, and textural items must be correct without being trite; they are used to soften or harden the telling of parts of the story.

Your work is full of meaning and symbolism. Considerations of your topic influence even your color choices. Why is that so important in making the work authentic and unique?

For me, the mood of a piece dictates the correct color tones to use. My color choices are mainly somewhat muted, and this relates to the subject matter of my Visual Anthologies. Much of my work involves the retelling of the Holocaust in Eastern Europe during World War II. The deliberate use and the nonuse of colors is critical to the authenticity of the pieces. Many uniforms worn by concentration camp victims had a color patch of fabric that defined a grouping, whether Jew, homosexual, gypsy, or political dissident. There were even

different color combinations of patches that made distinctions within each of those groups. The color choices of fabrics and materials are placed within a piece to symbolically refer to the subject matter of the book. At times, it is important to not put specific colors in a piece. If survivors of the Holocaust viewed a piece in which I used the color yellow, the piece would be abhorrent because the color yellow, the color of the star they were forced to wear that distinguished them as Jews, evokes their nightmares and memories of their horrific experience. Color is a perfect medium for me to symbolize events and places, to jog memories, or to set the mood for a piece.

Judy Wilkenfeld's journal, 22, is a marvel of three-dimensional objects incorporated into a book form. This journal, completed with the intention of being a gift to her partner, has pages that are inches thick. Every element used is steeped in meaning.

Both a great deal of thought and a great deal of heart go into making your books so astonishingly beautiful and complex. Tell us about the internal process you go through as you work on a piece.

There is a process to my books, but you might be surprised to know that much of it can't be, and isn't, planned. I have come to accept that serendipitous events play a vital role in my works. The more I work on my books, the more I feel that there's a greater force going on and assisting me in the telling of the stories. I do not know necessarily what the piece will end up looking like, nor do I know where each object will end up when I find them. I do not sit and sketch out the pieces. The works and my process are dynamic. I go with the flow and allow the piece to dictate to me the direction it wishes to go. Research, inquiry, heart, humility, instinct, passion, reverence— all of these components work together or independently at different times as a piece progresses.

If you choose a subject matter that you are passionate about, then you will throw yourself fully into a piece. All my heart and soul goes into a piece because my artworks are expressions of those things or people who mean something important to me or that have a message that needs to be imparted.

When all of one's energy goes into a piece then the universe starts to assist. That's when I start to find bits and pieces, found objects, book pages and covers–whatever– items I may have purchased years before. I surround myself with era-appropriate music. I surround myself with as many sensory experiences pertinent to the subject matter. A piece can certainly overtake my life for the time I am involved in the making of it.

The passion, the energy, is what we call Bashert. in Yiddishkeit, a vernacular form of Judaism. Loosely translated, Bashert means "serendipity," but it's not quite that. Bashert really means things that "are meant to be;" it's the mystical side of life that most of us

do not experience in our lifetime. I embrace my findings and piece them together in the form of a book, using the colors, textures and materials as my instinct dictates. I have come to know and accept that my instinct is really a spiritual or mystical source guiding me in the right direction. We are working together. So it's not simply serendipitous. It's my reverence for the nature of things, for the way of the universe, for the experiences of lives and those who have come before me. It is for the experience of those for whom I am doing an anthology.

I guess this is where I liken my artist books and Visual Anthologies to personal journaling. For whom does one journal for but oneself? Maybe we may feel future generations may one day look at our journals and will understand who we were? Journaling or the making of books like mine will allow an insight into the history and culture of our time, what people and events were like. After all journaling the present is creating the history of the future.

The attention to detail on Judy Wilkenfeld's journal pages is astonishing and intentional. Carefully created vignettes live on the pages of these journals. Each layer has significance and is deliberately chosen for its content.

CHAPTER 6:

KEEPING THE FIRE BURNING: FUELING YOUR CREATIVITY

Just as a fire cannot burn without fuel or oxygen, an artist can lose the flame in the presence of a vacuum. We require fuel—that is, inspiration—from sources outside ourselves. Although we needs to expose ourselves to variety in color, light, and sound, to other ways of thinking and seeing, we also need a little breathing room, a way of making time for ourselves in the midst of everyday life. These two necessities allow us to keep the creative flame burning; even when it seems that only embers exist, a little self-care can ignite the coals into a wildfire once again.

In order to fuel our creativity, it may be that what we need as artists is a little bit of time doing something different from the ordinary, such as a date night with our creative self. Other times, it may be that we need a full-blown adventure, such as a trip to an art retreat so that we can breathe new life into our work and our spirit by learning to use a new medium. Networking with other artists and simply sharing time and

laughter with other creative souls can benefit us greatly. Simple things, such as new music, a trip to the library, or an online chat with an artistic friend can also add creative fuel without a great deal of effort or expense.

Misty Mawn created this page in her signature style; the pages in this journal are loosely bound in fabric and tied with ribbon.

This hand-painted box by Misty Mawn was designed to hold the journal shown on the facing page.

ARTIST DATES

Artist dates are not a new concept, but the phrase "artist date" is one that caught on after Julia Cameron published *The Artist's Way* in 1992. Artists have always sought out and set aside time for creative refueling. This refilling of the well is a necessity. Obvious places to fan the flames are museums, galleries, libraries, and bookstores, but plenty of other activities also offer opportunities to refresh the artistic eye: drives through the countryside; weekend trips to different locales, visits to ethnic neighborhoods in larger cities; attending concerts, dance performances, or plays; walks in the park; summer art fairs; visits to the homes of other artists. Although we gravitate naturally toward some of these activities, sometimes we need to make a concerted effort to seek out fresh sensory input.

In order to fuel our creativity, it may be that what we need as artists is a little bit of time doing something different than the ordinary—a date night with our creative self. Other times, it may be that we need a full-blown adventure, such as a trip to an art retreat, so that we can breathe new life into our work and our spirits by learning some new tricks. Networking with other artists and simply sharing time and laughter with other creative souls can benefit us greatly. Simple things, though, like new music, a trip to the library or a museum, or an online chat with an artistic friend can add creative fuel without a great deal of expense.

STARTING THE FIRE:

BLOGGING AND SOCIAL NETWORKING

Reading and writing blogs are wonderful ways for artists to connect and discuss their lives and their work. Social networking sites such as Facebook and Twitter offer opportunities for more networking. From these connections, friendships are formed and artist groups come into being. Many people and groups go on to meet in the "real world" to share a meal, conversation, and artistic inspiration. If you want to connect with other artists, blogging and social networking online can be useful.

These pages by Linda Moonwood incorporate various works of self-portraiture on backgrounds created using a variety of techniques. She adds layers by working onto the images and the surround.

INFORMAL EDUCATION

Numerous retreats and workshop venues offer art-journaling classes and related topics. (See the Resources section, page 122, for a list of some of these.) These include large-scale annual retreats, with 300 to 600 attendees taking classes over a three- or four-day time period, in classes of about fifteen to twenty-five people. Medium-size retreats of 150 to 300 attendees are becoming popular as well. At the other end of the spectrum are smaller venues, which are hosted by a single instructor teaching a weekend, two- or three-day workshop to a group of fourteen people. These venues are located across the United States and are often listed in the advertising section of mixed-media art magazines. Specially arranged trips to France, Italy, Greece, or Mexico are also becoming increasingly popular.

You can find out more information about these venues, large and small, through their websites; here, too, you'll find links to the instructors and to the artists who have attended them. These venues have avid followings, and attendees love them for their level of instructor contact and the opportunity to connect with like-minded souls.

Local art centers and community colleges often offer classes in basic painting, drawing, and printmaking, art forms that also have relevance in art journaling. Check out your local colleges and universities for classes, workshops, and contacts for similar educational offerings in the surrounding areas.

Online classes by internationally recognized instructors in art journaling can be taken for a fraction of the cost of a retreat. The trade-off is the loss of camaraderie and opportunities to create personal connections and make artist friends. You also miss out on enjoying the one-on-one contact with an instructor who's in the room with you as you learn techniques.

Linda Moonwood incorporates works of self-portraiture on backgrounds created using a range of techniques.

En los oscuros ojos
las estrellas tristes
corren
quieren cantar
yo te amo

LULU

She smiled mysteriously

ARTISTICO

so much time
darting

"Oh, not yet!"
She cried

MAKING TIME AND FINDING BALANCE

I've been an artist and a parent working full-time outside the home. I have also been an artist and a single parent working full-time outside the home. Currently, I'm a work-from-home artist, author, and workshop instructor and parent of three children ages three to eleven. I understand *busy*.

To make time for art, you have to *believe* that it's possible to make time for art. I've learned that if I'm waiting for unfettered time in which to create, hell might well freeze over before that time arrives. This realization taught me to work with the situation at hand, regardless of the time constraints and priorities.

In a management workshop at the university where I worked, I heard the following story: A time-management expert was speaking to a group. He placed a wide-mouth jar on the table in front of him and explained that the jar represented the amount of time each person had in his daily or weekly schedule. Next to the jar was a collection of fist-size rocks. He carefully filled the jar with the big rocks, until he couldn't fit anymore in then asked if the jar was full. The group responded, "Yes." Then the speaker placed a bowl of pea gravel on the table and added some to the jar. The gravel fit into the spaces between the rocks. He asked again if the jar was full. "Maybe," the audience members replied carefully.

The speaker brought out a small tub of sand and dumped the sand into the jar. The sand filled the spaces between the rocks and the

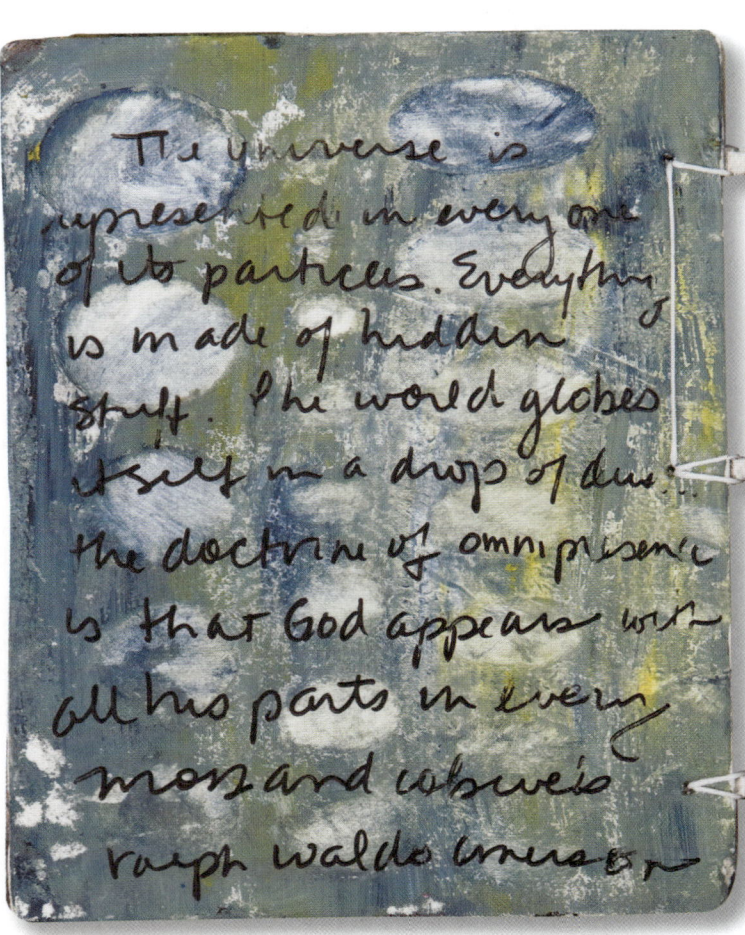

A collection of inspirational images, quotes, and writings form this journal by L.K. Ludwig.

gravel. Once more, he asked if the jar was full. "Probably not," replied the audience. Finally, the speaker took a pitcher of water and poured water into the jar until the jar was filled to the top. Then he looked at the group and asked: "What is the point of my demonstration?" One person replied: "To show that no matter how full your schedule is, you can always fit in one more thing."

"No," the time-management expert responded. The point of the demonstration is: "If you don't put the big rocks in first, they will never fit into the jar." What you have to decide is: *What are your big rocks?*

I learned more that day than I did at any management workshop in the eighteen years I worked in higher education. And what I learned made later decisions to change career paths much easier to face with confidence.

Note how you spend your time each day. List the activities in which you engage for a few days or a week, and see what you do with your free time. I easily decided what was most important—family, art, career—and made decisions about my time accordingly. I quickly realized that watching television

was time lost and not well spent. I learned that I spend a great deal of time online and made a guideline to be off the computer during set hours of the day so that my time went to my priorities, instead of into the ether. Give this exercise a try—chances are, you'll discover pockets of time to give to your art.

In this small, portable journal, photographs from adventures that were taken to refill my artistic well are incorporated along with inspirational.

KEEPER OF THE FLAME:

INSIGHTS FROM MISTY MAWN

Misty Mawn is a prolific artist and workshop instructor who works in paint and clay, on canvas and paper, and in journals, along with dabbling in digital work and creating videos. I asked Misty to speak about finding time for art.

I wear a few hats, but the two I wear constantly are mother and artist. Being a full-time mother and a full-time artist can be a lot to balance. Yes, there are those times when you lose your balance and fall flat on the floor, but you wipe it up while you are down there and gracefully get up. Then you accidentally wash your paintbrushes in the lunch dishwater, grab a pot of freshly brewed tea, and wipe the mouths of your dear children as you head to the studio, trying not to step on any LEGOS

or beads on the way. You check the clock to see how long you have before you need to consider what to make for dinner and then finally plop yourself down at your studio table, where you discover that someone has borrowed your scissors. You realize you've left your brushes in the kitchen, and now the dog is staring in from outside, wanting to be let in. Yes, that's a very typical five minutes in my life.

When there's little time to work, every minute counts, and this can be very frustrating when you're feeling blocked or uninspired. When this happens, instead of letting the frustration take its toll, I find that it's the perfect time to clean the studio, go for a walk with my camera, edit photos, blog or read blogs, or head out to the library with the kids and stock up on art books or music, anything that inspires. As an artist, I am constantly seeking inspiration and ways to improve, expand, or change my work. Visiting the library or bookstore to check out books and artist magazines is really all I have time for, right now, and for now, it's enough. There's always something I have yet to see or understand, even in children's art books where I find much inspiration.

There are times when it's a struggle to find the time to journal, explore who you are as an artist, and try new products and mediums

while doing what works best for everyone in your family. So, sometimes, doing what works is all you can do. That might mean turning your living room into a studio, getting takeout for dinner every so often, or staying up late to work and still getting up with everyone else in the morning. For me, late night is the best time to work. I feel the most creative at night; I can dive deeper into my work without the distractions that keep me from creating. Like most things in life, being a mother, wife, and artist is a dance—working together, the dance is so much more enjoyable.

Misty Mawn created this journal from what was originally loose pages inside a handpainted box. Using fabric as a book cover, the pages are gathered with ribbon.

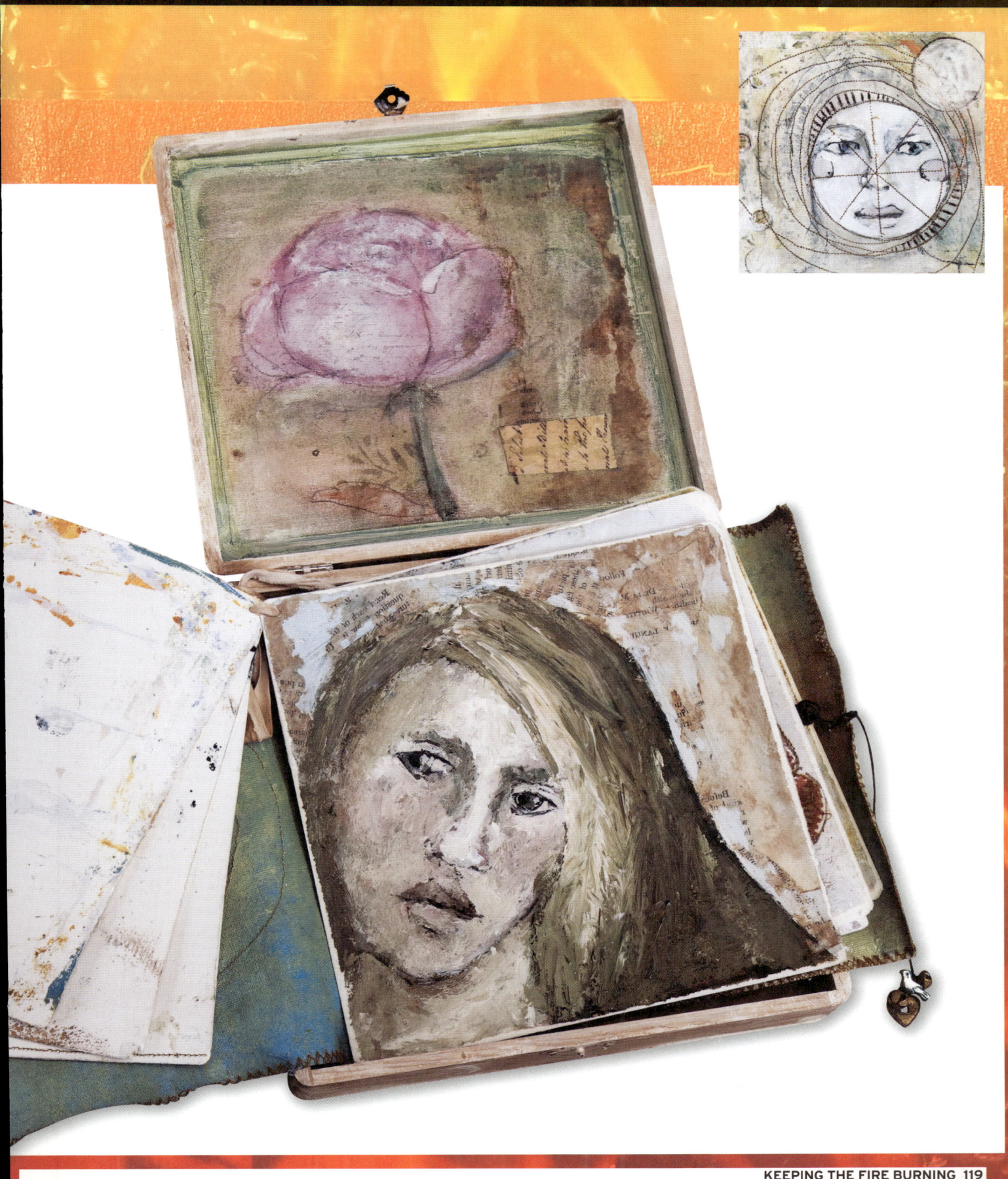

CONTRIBUTING ARTISTS

Tina Abbott
http://throughthekeyhole.typepad.com
Page 24

Seth Apter
http://thealteredpage.blogspot.com
Pages 100-101

Gina Armfield
http://sweetsistergina.typepad.com
Pages 60-61, 121, 125

Elizabeth Bunsen
http://elizabethbunsen.typepad.com
Pages 80-82

Karen Cole
http://karencole.blogspot.com
Pages 11, 96-97

Judi Delgado
www.bodhisartva.typepad.com
Pages 54-55, 56, 65

Pam Garrison
http://pamgarrison.typepad.com
Pages 44-45

John Hammons
http://johnhammons.blogspot.com
Pages 76, 77, 84, 89

Jan Harris
http://purplebirdart.blogspot.com
Pages 52-53, 102

Tracie Lyn Huskamp
http://thereddoor-studio.blogspot.com
Pages 87-88

Katie Kendrick
http://joyouslybecoming.typepad.com
Pages 48-51

L. K. Ludwig
http://gryphonsfeather.typepad.com/
Pages 46-47, 58-59, 64, 83, 123, 126-128

Liesel Lund
www.liesellund.com
Pages 72-75

Leslie Marsh
http://snipsandsnailsandpuppydogtails-leslie.blogspot.com
Page 99

Misty Mawn
www.mistymawn.typepad.com
Pages 85-86, 110-111, 118-119

Linda Moonwood
http://lulumoonmymuse.blogspot.com
Pages 112-115

Teesha Moore
www.teeshamoore.com
Pages 91, 92-93

Tracy Moore
www.sustainedconfusion.blogspot.com
Pages 90, 92

Mary Ann Moss
http://dispatchfromla.typepad.com
Pages 15, 42-43, 68

Brenda Beene Shackleford
http://betweenassignments.blogspot.com
Pages 14, 28-29, 38-39, 103

Judy Wilkenfeld
http://redvelvetcreations.blogspot.com
Pages 106-109

This journal page incorporates a pocket constructed of wire mesh that has been printed on using patina solution.

Gina Armfield used black-and-white self-portraiture integrated into pages rich with color to create soulful, meaningful content.

RETREA

PONDER

SILEN

EMBRACE

REST

RESOURCES

MORE BOOKS FROM QUARRY TO EXPLORE

Alphabetica, Lynne Perrella, Quarry Books, 2006

Altered Books, Collaborative Journals, and Other Adventures in Book Making, Holly Harrison, Quarry Books, 2005

Artist Journals and Sketchbooks: Exploring and Creating Personal Pages, Lynne Perrella, Quarry Books, 2005

Collaborative Art Journals and Shared Visions in Mixed Media, L. K. Ludwig, Quarry Books, 2003

Collage for the Soul, Holly Harrison, Quarry Books, 2003

Collage Lab: Experiments, Investigations, and Projects, Bee Shay, Quarry Books, 2010

The Complete Guide to Altered Imagery: Mixed-Media Techniques for Collage, Altered Books, Artist Journals, and More, Karen Michel, Quarry Books, 2005

Crafter's Devotional: 365 Days of Tips, Tricks, and Techniques for Unlocking Your Creative Spirit, Barbara Call, Quarry Books, 2009

Creative Paint Workshop for Mixed-Media Artists: Experimental Techniques for Composition, Layering, Texture, Imagery, and Encaustic, Ann Baldwin, Quarry Books, 2009

Drawing Lab for Mixed-Media Artists: 52 Creative Exercises to Make Drawing Fun, Carla Sonheim, Quarry Books, 2010

Fabric Art Journals: Making, Sewing, and Embellishing Journals from Cloth and Fibers, Pam Sussman, Quarry Books, 2005

Green Guide for Artists: Nontoxic Recipes, Green Art Ideas, & Resources for the Eco-Conscious Artist, Karen Michel, Quarry Books, 2009

Making Journals by Hand: 20 Creative Projects for Keeping Your Thoughts, Jason Thompson, Quarry Books, 2000

Making Memory Books by Hand: 22 Projects to Keep and Share, Kristina Feliciano, Quarry Books, 1999

Mixed Emulsions: Altered Art Techniques for Photographic Imagery, Angela Cartwright, Quarry Books, 2007

Mixed-Media Collage: An Exploration of Contemporary Artists, Methods, and Materials, Holly Harrison, Quarry Books, 2007

Mixed-Media Nature Journals: New Techniques for Exploring Nature, Life, and Memories, L. K. Ludwig, Quarry Books, 2008

Nature Inspired: Mixed-Media Techniques for Gathering, Sketching, Painting, Journaling, and Assemblage, Tracie Lyn Huskamp, Quarry Books, 2009

Playing with Books: The Art of Upcycling, Deconstructing, and Reimagining the Book, Jason Thompson, Quarry Books, 2010

Print & Stamp Lab: 52 Ideas for Handmade, Upcycled Print Tools, Traci Bunkers, Quarry Books, 2010

Re-Bound: Creating Handmade Books from Recycled and Repurposed Materials, Jeanine Stein, Quarry Books, 2009

True Vision: Authentic Art Journaling, L. K. Ludwig, Quarry Books, 2008

OTHER HELPFUL REFERENCE BOOKS

Keith Smith Books

Keith writes and publishes the best books on bookbinding out there. The following titles are available at www.keithsmithbooks.com and Amazon.com:

Non-Adhesive Binding, Volume I: Books Without Paste or Glue

Non-Adhesive Binding, Volume II: 1- 2- & 3-Section Sewings

Non-Adhesive Binding, Volume III: Exposed Spine Sewings

Non-Adhesive Binding, Volume IV: Smith's Sewing Single Sheets

Non-Adhesive Binding, Volume V: Quick Leather Bindings

MAGAZINES

Somerset Studio: www.stampington.com

Art Journaling: www.stampington.com

Cloth Paper Scissors: www.quiltingarts.com

Using photographs and collage on a painted surface, the author recorded images from a trip to California.

ART RETREATS

Artfest, Journalfest, PLAY
www.teeshamoore.com

Art & Soul
www.artandsoulretreat.com

Art Unraveled
www.artunraveled.com

Valley Ridge Art Studio
www.valleyridgeartstudio.com

ARTISTS TO RESEARCH

Peter Beard

Nancy Chunn

Dan Eldon

Sabrina Ward Harrison

Candy Jernigan

Fred Otnes

Robert Rauschenberg

ONLINE ART SUPPLY COMPANIES

Mister Art
www.misterart.com

Dick Blick
www.dickblick.com

Cheap Joe's Art Supply
www.cheapjoes.com

Pearl Paint
www.pearlpaint.com

GEL PENS

Jet Pens
www.jetpens.com

HANDBOUND JOURNALS

Rag and Bone Bindery
www.ragandbonebindery.com

BOOK BINDING SUPPLIES

Talas
www.talasonline.com

Volcano Arts
www.volcanoarts.biz

Royalwood Ltd. (waxed linen thread)
www.royalwoodltd.com

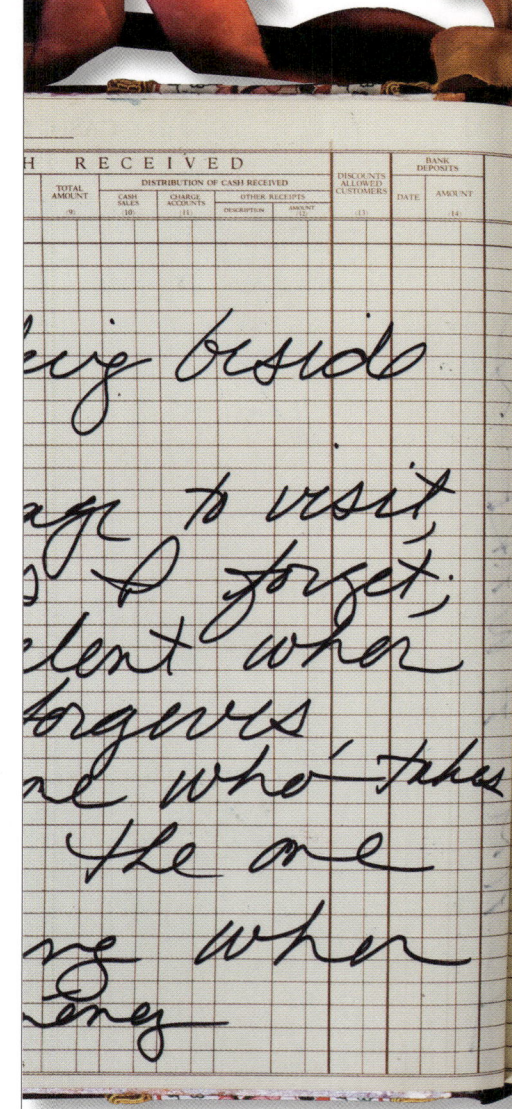

Using photographs and collage on a painted surface, the author recorded images from a trip to California.

ABOUT THE AUTHOR

L. K. Ludwig is an artist, photographer, author, and workshop instructor who lives, loves her family, and works in an old Victorian Foursquare in rural western Pennsylvania. She is the author of three books: *Mixed-Media Nature Journals; True Vision: Authentic Art Journaling*; and *Collaborative Art Journals* and *Shared Adventures in Mixed Media*. Weekends will often find her outdoors, playing and making art, at her family's weekend home on the banks of Allegheny River, where the natural world informs her work and infuses her spirit.

Photographic self-portraits taken while on teaching trips, were used on various journal pages.

ACKNOWLEDGMENTS

To my little loves, Gryphon, Maggie, and Sunny, and my beloved Joe: thank you for helping me fill my art journals with love, laughter, and adventure.

How he submitted—
Loved. Loved his
interior world,
his interior
wilderness, the primal
forest inside him,
where among decayed
tree trunks his
heart stood,
light green ...
Rainer Maria Rilke

may
apple